Reclaiming Your Life From a Traumatic Experience

Reclaiming Your Life From a Traumatic Experience

Workbook

Barbara Olasov Rothbaum • Edna B. Foa

• Elizabeth A. Hembree

OXFORD

UNIVERSITY PRESS

2007

OXFORD
UNIVERSITY PRESS

Oxford University Press, Inc., publishes works that further
Oxford University's objective of excellence
in research, scholarship, and education.

Oxford   New York
Auckland   Cape Town   Dar es Salaam   Hong Kong   Karachi
Kuala Lumpur   Madrid   Melbourne   Mexico City   Nairobi
New Delhi   Shanghai   Taipei   Toronto

With offices in
Argentina   Austria   Brazil   Chile   Czech Republic   France   Greece
Guatemala   Hungary   Italy   Japan   Poland   Portugal   Singapore
South Korea   Switzerland   Thailand   Turkey   Ukraine   Vietnam

Copyright © 2007 by Oxford University Press, Inc.

Published by Oxford University Press, Inc.
198 Madison Avenue, New York, New York 10016

www.oup.com

Oxford is a registered trademark of Oxford University Press

ISBN 978-0-19-530848-8 (pbk.)

9

Printed in the United States of America
on acid-free paper

Dedication

To my sister, Judy, and her husband, John. Not only do I love and cherish you and your friendship, but also you are my heroes for survival, resilience, grace under pressure, and working through adversity to emerge as stronger people.

—Barbara Olasov Rothbaum

To my daughters Yael and Michelle, who have always been supportive of my work even when it took me away from them, with much love and many thanks.

—Edna B. Foa

To Sam, Jessie, Ben, and Yoni—thank you for helping me keep it all in perspective.

—Elizabeth A. Hembree

About Treatments*ThatWork*™

One of the most difficult problems confronting patients with various disorders and diseases is finding the best help available. Everyone is aware of friends or family who have sought treatment from a seemingly reputable practitioner, only to find out later from another doctor that the original diagnosis was wrong or that the treatments recommended were inappropriate or perhaps even harmful. Most patients, or family members, address this problem by reading everything they can about their symptoms, seeking out information on the Internet, or aggressively "asking around" to tap knowledge from friends and acquaintances. Governments and health care policy makers are also aware that people in need do not always get the best treatments—something they refer to as "variability in health care practices."

Now health care systems around the world are attempting to correct this variability by introducing "evidence-based practice." This simply means that it is in everyone's interest that patients get the most up-to-date and effective care for a particular problem. Health care policy makers have also recognized that it is very useful to give consumers of health care as much information as possible so that they can make intelligent decisions in a collaborative effort to improve physical and mental health. This series, Treatments *ThatWork*™, is designed to accomplish just that. Only the latest and most effective interventions for particular problems are described in user-friendly language. To be included in this series, each treatment program must pass the highest standards of evidence available, as determined by a scientific advisory board. Thus, when individuals suffering from these problems or their family members seek out an expert clinician who is familiar with these interventions and decides that they are appropriate, they will have confidence that they are receiving the best care available. Of course, only your health care professional can decide on the right mix of treatments for you.

If you have experienced a trauma and have not been able to recover effectively on your own, this workbook can help. If you exhibit the symptoms of Posttraumatic Stress Disorder (PTSD), the tools and strategies outlined here will help you reduce your anxiety and fear, as well as any other trauma-related problems you may have. Through exposure exercises and emotional processing, you will learn that you can safely remember your trauma and the events surrounding it. Breathing techniques will help you tolerate your anxiety and decrease your feelings of distress. This program is most effectively applied by working in collaboration with your therapist.

David H. Barlow, Editor-in-Chief
Treatments *ThatWork*™
Boston, Massachusetts

Contents

Chapter 1   Introduction   *1*

Chapter 2   Is This Program Right for You?   *11*

Chapter 3   Session 1   *17*

Chapter 4   Session 2   *25*

Chapter 5   Session 3   *45*

Chapter 6   Anticipating and Solving Problems   *57*

Chapter 7   Intermediate Sessions   *65*

Chapter 8   Final Session   *71*

              About the Authors   *77*

Chapter 1   *Introduction*

Goals

- To understand the characteristics of Posttraumatic Stress Disorder (PTSD)

- To learn about Prolonged Exposure Therapy (PE)

- To learn how this program was developed

- To understand what the program will involve

What Is Posttraumatic Stress Disorder?

Posttraumatic stress disorder (PTSD) is an anxiety disorder that may develop after an event that is experienced or witnessed and involves actual or perceived threat to life or physical integrity. The person's emotional reaction to this event is characterized by horror, terror, or helplessness. As shown in table 1.1, people with PTSD have three major types of symptoms, which typically relate to:

- Reexperience of the trauma

- Avoidance of trauma reminders

- Hyperarousal

The symptoms of PTSD are common right after traumatic events, but for most trauma survivors, these symptoms decrease over time through natural recovery. However, for some people, the PTSD symptoms stay on, become chronic, and interfere with daily functioning. If this is true in your case, this program, based on Prolonged Exposure (PE) Therapy, can help.

Table 1.1 Symptoms of Posttraumatic Stress Disorder

Symptoms of Reexperiencing	Symptoms of Avoidance	Symptoms of Increased Arousal
Recurrent and intrusive distressing recollections of the event, including images, thoughts, or perceptions	Efforts to avoid thoughts, feelings, or conversations associated with the trauma	Difficulty falling or staying asleep
Recurrent distressing dreams of the event	Efforts to avoid activities, places, or people that arouse recollections of the trauma	Irritability or outbursts of anger
Acting or feeling as if the traumatic event were recurring (includes a sense of reliving the experience, illusions, hallucinations, and dissociative flashback episodes, including those that occur on awakening or when intoxicated)	Inability to recall an important aspect of the trauma	Difficulty concentrating
Intense psychological distress at exposure to internal or external cues that symbolize or resemble an aspect of the traumatic event	Markedly diminished interest or participation in significant activities	Hypervigilance
Physiological reactivity on exposure to internal or external cues that symbolize or resemble an aspect of the traumatic event	Feeling of detachment or estrangement from others	Exaggerated startle response
	Restricted range of affect (e.g., unable to have loving feelings)	
	Sense of foreshortened future (e.g., does not expect to have a career, marriage, children, or a normal life span)	

Source: American Psychiatric Association. (2000). *Diagnostic and statistical manual of mental disorders (4th ed.)—Text Revision.* Washington, DC: Author.

What Is Prolonged Exposure (PE) Therapy?

PE is a way to help trauma survivors to *emotionally process* their traumatic experiences. Doing this reduces PTSD and other trauma-related problems. The name Prolonged Exposure (PE) comes from the long tradition of exposure therapy for anxiety disorders. In exposure therapy clients are helped to confront safe but anxiety-arousing situations in order to decrease their excessive fear and anxiety. We are all familiar with the principles of exposure therapy. For example, a classic example of exposure is the advice to a rider to "get back on the horse" after being thrown off. In doing so, the rider overcomes her fear of being thrown again and prevents the fear from growing to excessive proportions.

At the same time, PE is rooted in the Emotional Processing Theory of PTSD. This theory emphasizes that special processing of the traumatic event must take place to help reduce PTSD symptoms. Throughout this workbook, we will emphasize emotional processing because it successfully reduces PTSD symptoms. We discuss Emotional Processing Theory in more detail in the section that follows.

The Prolonged Exposure treatment program includes the following procedures:

- Education about common reactions to trauma. You and your therapist will discuss common reactions that many people have, as well as your specific reactions.

- Breathing retraining, i.e., teaching you how to breathe in a calming way.

- Repeated in vivo ("in real life") exposure to situations or activities that you are avoiding because they remind you of your traumatic experience and make you anxious or distressed.

- Repeated, prolonged imaginal exposure to the trauma memories (i.e., revisiting the trauma in your imagination).

In vivo and imaginal exposures are the core of the treatment. These techniques were selected because there is a great deal of evidence showing that they effectively reduce anxiety and distress in people who suffer from anxiety disorders, such as specific phobias, panic disorder, social anxiety disorder, and obsessive compulsive disorder. As we discuss later in the chapter, 20 years of research have shown that PE is effective in reducing PTSD and other trauma-related problems such as depression, general anxiety, and anger. Obviously, there are no guarantees about how you will respond, but many, many people have been helped by this program, so we are hopeful that you will be too.

The aim of in vivo and imaginal exposure is to help you emotionally process the traumatic events by helping you face the memories of your trauma and the situations that are associated with these memories. This is a powerful way for you to learn that the memories of the trauma, and the situations or activities that are associated with these memories, are not the same as the trauma itself. You will learn that you can safely remember your trauma and experience the trauma reminders. The anxiety and distress that you feel at first will go down over time and you will be able to tolerate this anxiety. Ultimately, this treatment will help you reclaim your life from PTSD.

Prolonged Exposure Therapy is based on Emotional Processing Theory and was developed by Edna Foa and M. J. Kozak as a way to understand anxiety disorders and how exposure therapy reduces anxiety symptoms. Emotional Processing Theory is based on the idea that fear is represented in memory as a "program" for escaping danger. The fear structure includes different kinds of information, including information about what it is we are afraid of, called the feared stimuli (e.g., a bear), the fear responses (e.g., heart rate increases), and the meaning associated with the stimuli (e.g., bears are dangerous) and responses (e.g., fast heartbeat means I am afraid). When a fear is realistic we call it normal fear, and the fear structure contains information about how we can best respond to the real threat. So feeling fear or terror if we see a bear and acting to escape are appropriate responses and can be seen as a normal and helpful fear reaction.

According to Foa and Kozak, a fear structure becomes a problem when (1) the information in the structure does not accurately represent the world, (2) physical and escape/avoidance responses are triggered by harmless stimuli, (3) the fear responses interfere with daily functioning, and (4) harmless stimuli and responses are viewed as being dangerous. Foa and Kozak proposed that two conditions are necessary for successfully changing the unrealistic and abnormal fear structure, thereby reducing anxiety symptoms. First, the person's fear and anxiety need to be triggered or activated. If this is not done, the fear structure cannot be changed. Second, realistic information (e.g., talking about the traumatic experience and remembering that it did not cause me to break down) needs to replace the original, unrealistic information in the fear structure (e.g., I will fall apart if I allow myself to talk or think about the trauma). Exposure therapy meets these two conditions.

Sometimes, people also have thoughts that if they confront what they are scared of their anxiety will be so high that they will "lose control" or "go crazy." But research has shown that when they confront what they are scared of in a therapeutic manner, it helps these thoughts go away as well. Dr. Foa and her colleagues have published a number of papers describing how this treatment helps people with PTSD.

You may wonder why some trauma survivors develop PTSD and some do not. Within the framework of Emotional Processing Theory, the development of chronic PTSD is caused by the failure to fully process the traumatic memory. So the goal of therapy for PTSD is to promote emotional processing. Exposure to feared stimuli results in the activation (bringing to mind) of the relevant fear structure and at the same time provides realistic information about the likelihood and cost of the consequences you fear. In addition to the fear of external threat (e.g., being attacked again), the person may have unhelpful or inaccurate beliefs about anxiety itself that are disconfirmed during exposure, such as the belief that anxiety will never end until the situation is escaped or that the anxiety will cause the person to "lose control" or "go crazy." This new information is learned during the exposure therapy session, which changes the fear structure and causes the person to be less afraid the next time he or she faces that situation, and thereby results in a reduction of PTSD symptoms.

Prolonged Exposure for the treatment of PTSD works through bringing to mind the fear structure, deliberately confronting trauma-related thoughts and images, imaginal and in vivo exposure, and learning that what you were afraid of is very unlikely to happen.

By confronting trauma memories and reminders, people learn that they can tolerate these situations and that nothing bad happens to them. They also learn that their anxiety will decrease even while they are confronting what they fear. People learn that they don't go crazy or lose control. Imaginal and in vivo exposure exercises help you tell the difference between the traumatic event and other similar but non-dangerous events. This allows you to see the trauma as a specific event occurring in space and time, which helps you get over your feelings and thoughts that the world is entirely dangerous and that you are completely incompetent to deal with it. Importantly, people with PTSD often report that thinking about the traumatic event makes it feel as if it is happening all over again. Repeated imaginal exposure to the trauma memory helps people tell the difference between the past and present. It helps them realize that although remembering the trauma can be emotionally upsetting, the trauma is not happening again and therefore thinking about the event is not dangerous. Repeated imaginal exposure also helps people think differently about what happened to them. For example, someone who feels guilty about not having done more to resist an attacker may soon realize that the assault might have been more severe if she had resisted. All of these changes reduce PTSD symptoms and bring about a sense of mastery and competence. In each session following the imaginal exposure, you will talk with your therapist about the experience and how you are thinking and feeling about it and how that changes over time. This "processing" also helps change your fear structure.

How Was the Program Developed?

The PE treatment program was developed by the authors at the Center for the Treatment and Study of Anxiety (CTSA) at the University of Pennsylvania. Over the last 20 years we have conducted well-controlled studies in which we provided this treatment to hundreds of clients. In addition, we have trained many therapists in various settings and countries to use this treatment. Our clinical experiences and the results of our studies have guided the evolution of PE to its current form, which is detailed in the chapters that follow. PE has worked well in studies that were conducted at universities and when delivered by therapists in community agencies in the United States and around the world, including Israel, Japan, Australia, and Europe. Dr. Foa has been training therapists worldwide to use this therapy and is continuing to train more therapists.

As a result of the large body of research supporting the effectiveness of PE, the treatment program was given a 2001 Exemplary Substance Abuse Prevention Program Award by the U.S. Department of Health and Human Services, Substance Abuse and Mental Health Services Administration (SAMHSA), and was designated as a Model Program for national dissemination. We are very excited about how much PE helps people, and that is part of why we wrote this book—to help more people use it.

Risks and Benefits of This Treatment Program

Benefits

Twenty years of research on PE have yielded findings that clearly support the effectiveness of PE as a treatment for PTSD. Nearly all studies have found that PE reduces not only PTSD but also other trauma-related problems, including depression and general anxiety. It helps people to reclaim their lives.

Risks

The primary risks associated with PE therapy are discomfort and emotional distress, especially when confronting anxiety-provoking images, memories, and situations in the course of treatment. PE is designed to get you in touch with these emotions and reactions, and we know that it is often painful, especially at first. That is why it is best to do PE with the help of a trained therapist who will be there to help you through it. You may feel worse before you feel better. But, if you stick with it, the chances are excellent that you will feel much better in the long run. It is worth it!

Alternative Treatments

In addition to PE and other versions of exposure therapy, the CBT (cognitive behavioral therapy) programs that have been found effective include stress inoculation training (SIT), cognitive processing therapy (CPT), cognitive therapy (CT), and eye movement desensitization and reprocessing (EMDR).

The Role of Medications

Zoloft and Paxil are the only medications approved by the U.S. Food and Drug Administration (FDA) for use in treating PTSD. It is common for people already taking either of these drugs or other appropriate medication for PTSD and/or depression to enter therapy. If you are already taking these medications but still suffer from PTSD, you can stay on the medication and go through the PE program because we have not found the medication to interfere with this treatment.

Outline of This Treatment Program

The treatment program consists of 10–12 weekly or twice-weekly treatment sessions that are generally 90 minutes each. This workbook is divided into chapters that talk about what will happen in each session.

Each chapter includes the techniques you will use and how to use them, home exercises, and all necessary handouts and forms. Each session should be audiotaped for you to review as part of homework each session. In addition, a separate audiotape will be made during the breathing retraining in session 1 for you to use at home to practice the breathing relaxation. Finally, beginning in session 3, separate tapes of your imaginal exposure will be made for you to listen to once a day at home. Thus, two tapes are used in any session including imaginal exposure: the "session tape" records everything up to the beginning of your imaginal exposure, at which point the therapist will switch to a new audiotape to record only the imaginal exposure, and then will return to the session audiotape to record the discussion that follows the exposure exercise.

Structure of Sessions

Session 1 begins by presenting you with an overview of the treatment program and a general rationale for prolonged exposure. The second part of the session is devoted to collecting information about the trauma, your reactions to the trauma, and other stressful experiences you may have had. The session ends with the introduction of breathing retraining. For homework, you will be asked to review the Rationale for Treatment and practice the breathing retraining on a daily basis.

Session 2 presents you with an opportunity to talk in detail about your reactions to the trauma and its effect on you. Common reactions to trauma are discussed in this workbook. Next, your therapist will present the rationale for exposure, with an emphasis on in vivo exposure. Finally, during session 2, you and your therapist will construct a hierarchy of situations or activities and places that you are avoiding. After this session you will begin confronting situations for homework using in vivo exposure methods. Session 2 ends with your therapist assigning specific in vivo exposures for homework. You will also be encouraged to continue using the breathing exercises you learned in session 1 throughout the day when you feel anxious and to read the Common Reactions to Trauma information daily.

Session 3 begins with homework review. Your therapist will explain the rationale for imaginal exposure, or revisiting and recounting the trauma memory using your imagination. With your therapist's support and guidance, you will then experience your first imaginal revisiting of the trauma memory. During this exposure, you will be asked to visualize and describe the trauma memory for 45–60 minutes. This is followed by 15–20 minutes of discussion aimed at helping you to continue processing your thoughts and feelings about the trauma. Your homework for this session is to listen to the audiotape of the imaginal exposure and to continue with your in vivo exposure exercises.

Sessions 4–9 (or more) consist of homework review, followed by imaginal exposure, postexposure processing of thoughts and feelings, and discussion of your in vivo homework assignments. As treatment advances, you are encouraged to describe the trauma in much more detail during the imaginal exposure and to gradually focus more and more on the most distressing aspects of the trauma experience, or memory "hot spots." In later sessions, as you improve, the time dedicated to imaginal exposure will decrease to about 30 minutes.

Session 10 (or the *Final Session)* includes homework review, imaginal exposure, discussion of this exposure (with emphasis on how the experience has changed over the course of therapy), and a detailed review of your progress in treatment. The final part of the session is devoted to discussing continued practice of all that you learned in treatment, relapse prevention, and, if you are terminating therapy, saying goodbye to your therapist.

You have chosen to take back your life, and you are on the way!

Chapter 2

Is This Program Right for You?

Goals

- To determine if this program is right for you

- To enhance your motivation for treatment

Who Is Prolonged Exposure Therapy For?

Not every trauma survivor needs a trauma-focused treatment like PE. Many studies have shown that natural recovery works very well for many people who experience a traumatic event. In fact, PTSD symptoms and other trauma reactions are very common and happen for almost everyone right after a trauma, but then they decrease a lot for many people, especially over the first 3 months.

If at least a month has passed since you have experienced the traumatic event and you are still suffering from PTSD symptoms that are interfering with your life, it is time to think about seeking PE treatment. On the basis of treating and studying hundreds of trauma survivors, we recommend that you consider treatment with PE if:

- *You have PTSD and related problems (e.g., depression, chronic anxiety, high levels of anger or shame) following a trauma.*

- *You have a clear enough memory of the traumatic event(s) that you have a story of it:* you can imagine it and describe the traumatic memory (verbally or in writing), and the story has a beginning, middle, and end.

We do not recommend treatment with PE if:

- *You have strong urges and a plan to commit suicide or to harm other people or if you have recently attempted such behaviors.* While feeling suicidal and having a history of suicide gestures or attempts are quite common in people with PTSD, if suicidal plans or intentions are current, we recommend that you address them in treatment first. Studies have shown that PE reduces symptoms of depression as well as PTSD, but you have to be feeling strong enough and committed to staying alive in order to achieve these benefits. If you have doubts or concerns about this, you should definitely discuss them with your therapist so that you can together make decisions about treatment focus and how and when to proceed with PE.

- *You are engaging in serious self-injurious behavior.* It is also not unusual for some people with PTSD to have histories of cutting or burning or otherwise hurting themselves on purpose. However, if this is currently going on, you should not start PE until you are able to manage the impulses to hurt yourself without acting on them. If this has been a way that you have coped with emotional pain in the past, then during treatment you may have increased urges to harm yourself. But doing so is not an option during treatment with PE, as you need to learn that you can tolerate these negative emotions and that they will decrease without efforts to escape, avoid, or distract.

- *You have a current, high risk of being assaulted or abused (e.g., you are living with an abusive spouse, partner, or some other person who is physically hurting you).* If you are currently in a living situation in which you are being beaten, sexually assaulted, or seriously harmed, this must be the first focus of any help you receive. Your safety is absolutely most important. PE or any treatment for past traumas should be delayed until you are safely away from this ongoing violence.

- *You do not have sufficient memory of the traumatic event(s).* PE should not be used as a means of helping someone retrieve or remember a traumatic event. While people do sometimes remember more details of a trauma through the course of PE, we strongly discourage its use with people who have only a "sense" or a vague feeling that they suffered a trauma that is not remembered. If this describes what you feel, then we recommend that you discuss it with your therapist. The therapist can help you deal with these feelings but should not try to use imaginal exposure to pull for or help you to recover memories.

Other issues to consider when deciding if you are a good candidate for PE:

Presence of Drug and/or Alcohol Abuse and Dependence

In our early studies, we usually recommended that people with drug or alcohol problems seek treatment for the drug- and alcohol-related disorders first and then return for trauma-focused therapy. We have modified this practice over recent years and now offer PE to PTSD sufferers with current drug and alcohol abuse. We even have some preliminary evidence from an ongoing study that people with chronic PTSD and alcohol dependence benefit from PE, while getting treatment for their alcohol dependence at the same time. But we do often see alcohol and substance use as a form of avoidance and strongly encourage people to stop the alcohol or substance use, with the aid of AA or NA and other available supports. We monitor the substance abuse throughout treatment and are especially watchful for its use as a way to decrease or avoid anxiety and other painful feelings.

You probably know whether you are using alcohol or drugs to block out distressing, trauma-related feelings and thoughts. You probably also know that such abuse may eventually bring about a whole host of other problems in life. If you are going to use PE to deal with your trauma-related problems, it is important that you think about whether you use alcohol and/or drugs to avoid or block out painful thoughts and feelings and that you discuss this with your therapist. It may be helpful to seek additional help or support to reduce or stop your use of substances.

Living or Working in a High-Risk Environment

It is reasonable to question whether PE will be effective for someone who lives in a very dangerous area or has a hazardous job that carries a significant risk of harm. Unfortunately, examples of this are plentiful: the person living with the threat of terrorist attacks in Israel or war-torn countries, the woman living in an impoverished and violent neighborhood next door to a crack house, and the active-duty marine who will soon be deployed overseas for another tour of duty in a dangerous land.

Can PE help people whose life circumstances make it likely that they may be exposed to more traumas in the future or even during their treatment? Our experiences both in the United States and abroad have taught us that the answer to this question is often yes. If you have PTSD, then a big part of the fear and avoidance you are experiencing is due to events that happened to you in the past. While this fear may be fueled by the present-day risk of harm, the reverse is also usually true: the presence of PTSD is likely amplifying or worsening your fear of harm in day-to-day life. This disorder makes people very afraid in their present lives. You and your therapist will do your best to plan your in vivo exposure exercises so that they will be useful to your recovery but not carry a high risk of harm or danger. We think that when the PTSD symptoms related to your past trauma are reduced, you will be better able to address how you can live your life more comfortably given the day-to-day stresses and dangers you may face.

In summary, most individuals with PTSD (or severe, clinically significant symptoms of PTSD) following all types of trauma and who have a clear memory of their traumatic experience(s) are potentially good candidates for PE. Other problems, as well as multiple life difficulties (e.g., unemployment, financial difficulties, chronic health problems, relationship and family troubles, social isolation, to name a few), are extremely common in people with chronic PTSD. You may be suffering from some of these problems yourself. In general, we recommend that if a disorder other than PTSD is present that is life threatening or otherwise causing problems, it should be treated before you try PE.

Enhancing Motivation for Treatment

It is difficult for people suffering from PTSD to confront feared and avoided memories and reminders of traumatic experiences. The dropout rate from exposure therapy is no different than that of other active forms of CBT for PTSD, but nonetheless, 20–30% of PTSD clients do terminate treatment prematurely. Avoidance is part of PTSD, and people often struggle with urges to avoid throughout treatment. You may experience this, too, and your therapist will understand and even expect this. He or she will most likely discuss it with you and help you over the avoidance hurdles as they come up.

If you find that you are struggling with whether it is worth it to deal with your trauma and try to recover from PTSD and are not sure if you want to go through this program now, we think it is helpful for you to consider a few important questions: (1) What areas of your life have been disrupted or are unsatisfying as a result of the trauma? (2) What are some potential gains or positive changes that will result from therapy or from reducing PTSD symptoms and related interference? (3) What are some likely obstacles to successful therapy (e.g., difficulties attending therapy sessions, finding time to do homework, finding a tape player to listen to audiotapes or the privacy to listen to them, etc.)? and (4) What do you need to help find the motivation for therapy or to give yourself permission to do this now?

If the trauma was recent enough that you can remember life before and after the trauma, think about how the PTSD is controlling your life now. What things that you used to enjoy can you not do anymore or not do without a lot of anxiety? Other useful areas to think about:

■ Are there things that your friends or other people are able to do that you do not do now?

■ What would you like to change in your life now? What do you wish you could do at the end of therapy or 6 months from now?

■ Have you tried to get help for this in the past? What was it like? Did it help you? If not, why not? What made it difficult for you? If you did not complete treatment, what made you decide to quit?

■ Some people going through PE feel worse before they feel better, and their symptoms may increase before heading down. Given what you know about yourself, if this happens, how will it be for you? Is there anything your therapist can do to help you tolerate this temporary worsening?

■ PE requires time and effort. The homework is an important part of the process. Is there anything that may get in the way of your being able to do this?

■ Sometimes there are aspects of people's lives that actually change for the *better* after a trauma. Is this true for you, and if so, what do you feel you have gained from experiencing the trauma?

■ Although PE is often really effective in helping people get their lives back, it also can be stressful and may sometimes be time intensive and demanding. Will the effort of therapy be worthwhile for you? What will happen in your life if you don't work on these problems?

Finally, some clients have worried about how their therapist will handle the impact of hearing such detailed descriptions of traumatic events. They worry about the therapist and his or her reactions to what they describe. While the concern is appreciated, it is not good for treatment. Please rest assured that your therapist is able to handle whatever you have to say. He or she is there to take care of you. Although PE will be challenging at times for you and your therapist, it is very rewarding for both as well. We have had clients come back after therapy and tell us that they feel like the people they were before the trauma and that they had not thought that was possible. PE has allowed us to witness the resilience of the human spirit. We wish you the same!

Chapter 3

Session 1

Goals

- To learn about the treatment program and the procedures that will be used

- To complete the Trauma Interview with your therapist

- To learn a brief breathing retraining relaxation technique

Overview of Program and Treatment Procedures Used

The main tools of this therapy program are imaginal and in vivo exposure. You and your therapist will discuss why this therapy is important for you and how it will be tailored to you and your specific trauma-related symptoms and concerns. You will have the chance to ask questions and make sure you understand why you are being asked to relive the painful memories of your traumatic experience and how you can do it effectively to help make them less painful.

Some people who have been through traumatic experiences tell us that they have tried and failed to face their fears or that they did face them but their anxiety did not decrease. Some just cannot picture themselves doing some things they have been avoiding or being strong enough to picture and describe traumatic memories. Have you had thoughts like this? If so, share them with your therapist; she won't be surprised to hear them. In this session, you and your therapist will discuss how this therapy makes sense for you and the problems you are experiencing and how it will be different from how you have approached your memories in the past.

This treatment program consists usually of 10 to 12 90-minute sessions but occasionally can take up to 15 sessions in total. You will meet once or twice per week with your therapist, so the therapy will be completed in about 2 or 3 months. In this program, you are going to focus on the fears that you are experiencing and on your problems coping, both of which are directly related to your traumatic experience(s). Although often posttrauma reactions gradually get better with time, for many survivors like you, some of these symptoms continue to cause distress. It is helpful for your recovery process to understand what maintains posttrauma problems.

A major factor that maintains your trauma-related difficulties is *avoidance* of situations, memories, thoughts, and feelings that are related to your traumatic experiences. There are two ways that people avoid dealing with trauma reminders. The first is trying to push away images and feelings about the trauma. The second is escaping or avoiding situations, places, people, and activities that cause distress and fear because they are similar to the trauma or are reminders of the trauma. However, while the strategy of avoiding trauma-related thoughts and situations works in the short run, it actually prolongs the posttrauma reactions and prevents you from getting over your trauma-related difficulties. Can you think of things that you have avoided since the trauma? It is helpful to write them down and talk about them with your therapist.

Because avoiding thoughts about the trauma and situations that remind you of the trauma maintains your PTSD, Prolonged Exposure Therapy encourages you to face your trauma-related thoughts and situations as a way of helping you to deal with them. The treatment includes two types of confrontations or exposures. The first one is called *imaginal exposure,* in which we will ask you to revisit the traumatic experience and recount it aloud. The goal of imaginal exposure is to help you to process the traumatic memory by asking you to repeatedly face the memory during your sessions. We have found that repeated and prolonged (up to 45 minutes) imaginal exposure to the traumatic memory is quite effective in reducing trauma-related symptoms and helps you to think about it differently.

The second type of exposure is called *in vivo exposure,* which just means exposure "in real life." Here we will ask you to gradually approach situations that you have been avoiding because they remind you of the trauma, directly or indirectly (e.g., driving a car, walking alone in safe place, or lighting a fire in the fireplace). In vivo exposure is very effective in reducing excessive fears and avoidance after a trauma. If you avoid trauma-related situations that are objectively safe, you do not give yourself the chance to get over your fear of these situations. This is because until you face these situations, you may continue to believe that they are dangerous and that your anxiety in these situations will remain forever. However, if you face these situations in a gradual, systematic way, you will find out that they are not actually dangerous and that your anxiety will go down with repeated, prolonged confrontations. Does the idea of exposure make sense to you?

A second factor that maintains your posttrauma reactions is *the presence of unhelpful, disturbing perceptions, thoughts, and beliefs.* These disturbing perceptions and beliefs may be about the world in general, other people, yourself, or your reaction to the trauma. As a result of trauma, many people adopt the idea that the world is extremely dangerous. Therefore, even objectively safe situations are viewed as dangerous. Also, immediately after the trauma, many people adopt the view that they are incompetent and unable to cope, even with normal daily stressors. Trauma survivors may also blame themselves for the trauma and put themselves down because they are having difficulty coping after it. Engaging in or resuming daily activities and not avoiding trauma reminders help trauma survivors realize that the world is mostly safe and they are mostly competent. However, avoiding trauma reminders and developing PTSD often makes survivors continue to view the world as extremely dangerous and themselves as extremely incompetent and unable to cope. Does this sound familiar? Do you feel this way about yourself?

How do these excessively negative and unrealistic thoughts and beliefs about the world and about yourself maintain your posttrauma reactions? If you believe that the world is dangerous, you will continue to avoid even safe situations. Similarly, if you believe that the trauma is your fault, you may blame yourself and feel incompetent, and this will interfere with your ability to get back to your usual life. Likewise, if you believe that experiencing flashbacks is a sign that you are losing control, you may try very hard to push the traumatic memories out of your mind. However, the more you try to push these memories away, the more they will intrude on your consciousness and the less control you will actually have over the memories.

These disturbing thoughts and beliefs may be triggered during the repeated imaginal and in vivo exposure. But the revisiting and recounting of the traumatic event will give you the opportunity to gain a new, more realistic perspective about what happened and what it means to you now. We are going to try to make sense of a terrible situation, to give you a useful way to think about it.

You are going to work very hard, together with your therapist, during the next few weeks to help you get on with your life. Your work will be intensive, and you may find that you are experiencing discomfort as you face the things that remind you of your trauma. Your therapist may be available to talk with you between sessions if you feel that it would be helpful to you.

Information Gathering

At this point in the session, your therapist will ask you questions from the Trauma Interview to collect general information about your current problems and functioning, the traumatic experience(s), your physical and mental health since the trauma, social support, and use of alcohol and drugs.

We understand that answering specific and directive questions about the traumatic experience(s) and your reactions to the trauma may be difficult for you. However, this is an important step for you in your treatment, and your therapist needs to know what happened to you and how you have reacted to be able to help you. Be assured that therapists who are trained in this type of therapy and in helping people who have been through these types of experiences can handle it. He or she can also handle your reactions, so you are in good hands.

Breathing Retraining

After the interview, your therapist will teach you a brief breathing retraining relaxation technique before you leave the first session in order to help with any anxiety that may have been triggered by discussing the trauma. Most of us realize that our breathing affects the way that we feel. For example, when we are upset, people may tell us to take a deep breath and calm down. However, taking one deep breath often does not help. Instead, in order to calm down you should slow down your breathing by taking normal breaths and exhaling slowly. It is exhalation that is associated with relaxation, not inhalation. While you exhale, say the words *calm* or *relax* silently to yourself very slowly. Like this: *c-a-a-a-a-a-l-m*.

In addition to concentrating on slow exhalation while saying *calm* to yourself, we want you to try to slow down your rate of breathing. Very often, when people become frightened or upset, they feel like they need more air and may therefore hyperventilate. Hyperventilation, however, does not have a calming effect. In fact, it makes you feel more anxious. Unless we are preparing to fight or flee from real danger, we often do not need as much air as we are taking in when we are anxious. When we are anxious, we may hyperventilate, or over-breathe; this signals our bodies that we are getting ready to fight or flee and that we need extra oxygen in order to do so. This is similar to a runner taking deep breaths to fuel the body with oxygen before a race and continuing to breathe deeply and quickly throughout the race. Hyperventilating also produces bodily reactions that resemble fear. These bodily reactions, in turn, can make us more afraid. What we really need to do is to slow down our breathing and take in less air.

You will take a normal breath and exhale very slowly, saying the word *calm* or *relax* to yourself. Then you will pause and count to three or four before taking a second breath. Repeat the entire breathing sequence 10 to 15 times. Your therapist may make a tape of himself or herself directing you through these breathing exercises for you to practice with for homework. Please review the breathing retraining technique in the next section. You should practice this breathing technique three times a day, but you can also use it when you feel particularly tense or distressed throughout the day or to help you relax or go to sleep at night.

Breathing Retraining Technique

Purpose of Exercises

■ Slow down breathing

■ Decrease amount of oxygen in blood

■ With practice, decrease anxiety

Breathing Instructions

1. Take a normal breath in through your nose with your mouth closed.

2. Exhale slowly with your mouth closed.

3. On exhaling, silently say to yourself the word *calm* or *relax* very slowly; for example: *c-a-a-a-a-a-l-m* or *r-e-e-e-l-a-a-a-a-x*.

4. Pause, holding your breath, for a count of four, and then take the next inhalation.

5. Practice this exercise several times a day, for 10 minutes each time.

Listening to Session Tapes

Your therapist will audiotape all of your sessions and give you the session tape to listen to as part of your homework between sessions. Many clients have found this a useful experience. It gives you an opportunity to think about and process information you received and the discussion you had with your therapist. This is often very helpful, as we process information differently when we are not actively engaged in a conversation. In several weeks, when you begin revisiting and recounting your trauma memory in session, your therapist will also make you a separate tape of this imaginal exposure to listen to at home.

Homework

✎ Practice breathing retraining for 10 minutes, three times a day.

✎ Listen to the audiotape of this session one time.

✎ Read the Rationale for Treatment found at the end of this chapter. You may share it with people who are close to you if you think it will help them understand what you are going through.

Rationale for Treatment by Prolonged Exposure

The treatment program you are participating in is called Prolonged Exposure. There are two main parts to this program.

The first is **imaginal exposure,** in which you relive the trauma repeatedly in your mind. The second part is **in vivo exposure,** in which you confront safe situations that you have been avoiding because you became afraid of them after your trauma. Many people who have experienced a trauma try to avoid thoughts and feelings associated with that event. Similarly, many people also avoid situations, places, and activities that remind them of the trauma or that just feel scary. However, while avoiding can make you feel more comfortable in the short run, it actually can make the problem worse in the long run, because it prevents you from overcoming your fears. Imaginal and in vivo exposure address these problems and work in similar ways.

How does exposure work? When you confront feared memories or situations in a systematic way under relatively safe circumstances, several things happen. One, reliving the memory helps to emotionally process the traumatic experience and make sense of it. Two, you learn that thinking about a traumatic experience is not dangerous and that being upset or anxious is not dangerous. Three, you become less fearful of other situations that remind you of your trauma. Four, you learn that you can handle your fear and anxiety, and you feel better about yourself. Finally, you learn that when you repeatedly confront memories or situations you have avoided, the fear and distress gradually decrease. In other words, you again become relatively comfortable in these situations. We call this *habituation*. Habituation is the process by which anxiety comes down on its own. When you stick it out and stay in a frightening but safe situation for a long enough time and you go back to that same situation often enough, you simply become less frightened of this situation. In a way, it is similar to "getting back on a bicycle" after falling off. If you refuse to try again, over time you become more and more frightened of riding bicycles. But if you force yourself to ride them despite your fear, you become less afraid.

Habituation works with frightening memories, too. Letting yourself engage in the traumatic memories rather than avoiding them will allow you to remember the trauma with less distress, and you will learn that the memories are not dangerous. Exposure to the painful memories, i.e., reliving the trauma in imagination, also allows you to gain control over them so they will be less likely to pop up at times you do not want them to. The flashbacks, nightmares, and intrusive thoughts that many trauma survivors often experience are less likely to occur after you repeatedly relive the trauma, and when they do occur, they are less upsetting.

Following a trauma, people's beliefs about themselves and about the world may change in basic ways. You may view situations as dangerous when before the trauma they would not have bothered you at all. You may find that your attitude toward people and in general has become more negative than it used to be, or that your self-image has gotten worse. Many times these changes reflect trauma-related changes in your thinking. Sometimes even the presence of posttraumatic stress disorder may cause you to think and feel negatively about yourself. Because how you think about yourself, the world, and other people affects how you feel, it is useful to pay attention to how the traumatic experience has shaped your thoughts and beliefs. For this reason, as you go through the treatment, you and your therapist will discuss how you think about the trauma, yourself, other people, and situations in your life. You will sometimes explore trauma-related changes in your thinking in order to see how they affect your feelings and whether they are helpful or not.

Treatment by imaginal and in vivo exposure may seem difficult at first, and many trauma survivors are afraid of becoming involved in it. But with time you will find that this treatment is challenging and makes you feel good about yourself. Congratulations! You have made the very scary first step in taking back control of your life!

Chapter 4

Session 2

Goals

- To review homework

- To learn about the common reactions to trauma

- To review the rationale for exposure therapy, especially for in vivo exposure

- To learn about the Subjective Units of Discomfort Scale (SUDS)

- To create your in vivo exposure hierarchy

- To choose in vivo assignments for homework

Overview

In session 2, you and your therapist will discuss the usual/common reactions that people have after they experience a traumatic event, as well as your personal experience of these reactions. Your therapist will explain to you why in vivo exposure works, and you will work together to construct a list of safe or low-risk situations that you have been avoiding and that are important for you to confront again. After this session, you will begin your in vivo exposure practice. You will confront situations in real life ("in vivo") that you avoid or that, if you can't entirely avoid them, you try to bear as briefly as possible. Most of your in vivo exposure practices will be done between sessions as homework exercises. However, sometimes your in vivo exposure might include situations or things that can be practiced during your therapy session, such as greeting men or making eye contact with them, lying on your back with your eyes closed, sitting in a waiting room with unfamiliar people, sitting at a table in a cafeteria by yourself or with your back to others, etc. If it seems useful, these situations may be first practiced in the therapy session with your therapist.

Homework Review

At the beginning of the session, you and your therapist will discuss how you have been doing in the past week and about your reactions to the first session. Your therapist will review the questionnaires you filled out before the session to see how your mood and symptoms have been during the last week.

Discussion about the Common Reactions to Trauma

The common reactions to trauma discussion has several aims:

- To help you share your own experience of PTSD symptoms and related problems and give you information about these reactions.

- To help you to understand your symptoms and reactions by putting them into context.

- To give you hope by helping you realize that many of your problems are directly related to PTSD and that many of them will improve with this treatment.

You will spend a large part of this session talking with your therapist about the common reactions to trauma. Please review the Common Reactions to Trauma information included here after the session as part of your homework.

Common Reactions to Trauma

A traumatic experience is an emotional shock and may cause many emotional problems. This section describes some of the common reactions people have after a trauma. Because everyone responds differently to traumatic events, you may have some of these reactions more than others, and some you may not have at all.

Remember, many changes after a trauma are normal. In fact, most people who directly experience a major trauma have severe reactions in the immediate aftermath. Many people then feel much better within 3 months after the event, but others recover more slowly, and some do not recover enough without help. Becoming more aware of the changes you have undergone since your trauma is the first step toward recovery.

Some of the most common problems after a trauma are described below.

1. **Fear and anxiety**. Anxiety is a common and natural response to a dangerous situation. For many people it lasts long after the trauma has ended. This happens when one's views of the world and sense of safety have changed and become more negative. You may become anxious when you remember the trauma. But sometimes anxiety may come from out of the blue. **Triggers or cues** that can cause anxiety may include places, times of day, certain smells or noises, or any situation that reminds you of the trauma. As you begin to pay more attention to the times you feel afraid, you can discover the triggers for your anxiety. In this way, you may learn that some of the out-of-the-blue anxiety is really triggered by things that remind you of your trauma.

2. **Reexperiencing the trauma.** People who have been traumatized often reexperience the traumatic event. For example, you may have **unwanted thoughts** of the trauma and find yourself unable to get rid of them. Some people have **flashbacks**, or very vivid images, as if the trauma is occurring again. **Nightmares** are also common. These symptoms occur because a traumatic experience is so shocking and so different from everyday experiences that you can't fit it into what you know about the world. So in order to understand what happened, your mind keeps bringing the memory back, as if to better digest it and fit it in.

3. **Increased arousal** is also a common response to trauma. This includes feeling jumpy, jittery, and shaky; being easily startled; and having trouble concentrating or sleeping. Continuous arousal can lead to **impatience** and **irritability**, especially if you're not getting enough sleep. The arousal reactions are due to the fight or flight response in your body. The fight or flight response is how we protect ourselves against danger, and it also occurs in animals. When we protect ourselves from danger by fighting or running away, we need a lot more energy than usual, so our bodies pump out extra adrenaline to help us get the extra energy we need to survive.

   People who have been traumatized often see the world as filled with danger, so their bodies are on constant alert, always ready to respond immediately to any attack. The problem is that increased arousal is useful in truly dangerous situations, such as if we find ourselves facing a tiger. But alertness becomes very uncomfortable when it continues for a long time even in safe situations. Another reaction to danger is to **freeze**, like the deer in the headlights, and this reaction can also occur during a trauma.

4. **Avoidance** is a common way of managing trauma-related pain. The most common is avoiding situations that remind you of the trauma, such as the place where it happened. Often situations that are less directly related to the trauma are also avoided, such as going out in the evening if the trauma occurred at night. Another way to reduce discomfort is to try to push away painful thoughts and feelings. This can lead to feelings of **numbness**, where you find it difficult to have both fearful and pleasant or loving feelings. Sometimes the painful thoughts or feelings may be so intense that your mind just blocks them out altogether, and you may not remember parts of the trauma.

5. Many people who have been traumatized feel **angry** and **irritable**. If you are not used to feeling angry, this may seem scary as well. It may be especially confusing to feel angry at those who are closest to you. Sometimes people feel angry because of feeling irritable so often. Anger can also arise from a feeling that the world is not fair.

6. Trauma often leads to feelings of **guilt** and **shame**. Many people blame themselves for things they did or didn't do to survive. For example, some assault survivors believe that they should have fought off an assailant, and they blame themselves for the attack. Others feel that if they had not fought back they wouldn't have gotten hurt. You may feel ashamed because during the trauma you acted in ways that you would not otherwise have done. Sometimes, other people may blame you for the trauma.

Feeling guilty about the trauma means that you are taking responsibility for what occurred. While this may make you feel somewhat more in control, it can also lead to feelings of helplessness and depression.

7. **Grief and depression** are also common reactions to trauma. This can include feeling down, sad, hopeless, or despairing. You may cry more often. You may lose interest in people and activities you used to enjoy. You may also feel that plans you had for the future don't seem

to matter anymore, or that life isn't worth living. These feelings can lead to thoughts of wishing you were dead, or doing something to hurt or try to kill yourself. Because the trauma has changed so much of how you see the world and yourself, it makes sense to feel sad and to grieve for what you lost because of the trauma.

8. **Self-image** and **views of the world** often become more negative after a trauma. You may tell yourself, "If I hadn't been so weak or stupid this wouldn't have happened to me." Many people see themselves as more negative overall after the trauma ("I am a bad person and deserved this").

   It is also very common to see others more negatively and to feel that you can't **trust** anyone. If you used to think about the world as a safe place, the trauma may suddenly make you think that the world is very dangerous. If you had previous bad experiences, the trauma may convince you that the world is dangerous and others aren't to be trusted. These negative thoughts often make people feel that they have been changed completely by the trauma. Relationships with others can become tense, and it may be difficult to become intimate with people as your trust decreases.

9. **Sexual relationships** may also suffer after a traumatic experience. Many people find it difficult to feel sexual or have sexual relationships. This is especially true for those who have been sexually assaulted, since in addition to the lack of trust, sex itself is a reminder of the assault.

10. Some people increase their **use of alcohol or drugs** after a trauma. There is nothing wrong with responsible drinking, but if your use of alcohol or drugs has increased as a result of your traumatic experience, it can slow down your recovery and cause problems of its own.

Many of the reactions to trauma are connected to one another. For example, a flashback may make you feel out of control and will therefore produce fear and arousal. Many people think that their common reactions to the trauma mean that they are "going crazy" or "losing it." These thoughts can make them even more fearful. Again, as you become aware of the changes you have gone through since the trauma and as you process these experiences during treatment, the symptoms should become less distressing.

In the first session with your therapist, you talked about confronting the memories of your traumatic experience with imaginal (in your imagination) exposure and in vivo (in real life) exposure and why they are helpful in recovering from the types of symptoms you are having. In this session, you and your therapist will review the rationale for in vivo exposure and talk about how confronting the situations you have been avoiding will help you overcome your PTSD. You will then begin to construct a list of situations that you've been avoiding, which will be good to practice for your in vivo exposure exercises.

Remember that it is common for people to want to escape or avoid memories, situations, thoughts, and feelings that are painful and upsetting. This avoidance of upsetting experiences may make you feel better in the short run, but in the long run avoidance just feeds posttrauma reactions and keeps you from recovering from PTSD.

There are several ways that in vivo exposure can help you get over your PTSD symptoms.

First, you now have a habit of lowering anxiety by avoiding situations that cause you to feel bad. For example, if you are at home and you discover that you ran out of milk, you may say to yourself, "I need to go to the supermarket to get some more milk." As you think this, you begin to feel very anxious. Then you may say to yourself, "I can wait for my husband to come home and shop for the milk." As soon as you make the decision not to go shopping, your anxiety goes down and you feel better. Each time you decrease your anxiety by avoidance, your habit of avoiding gets stronger and stronger. Carefully confronting the situations that you currently avoid will help you get over your habit of reducing anxiety through avoiding.

Second, when you put yourself in situations over and over that you have avoided because you thought that they were dangerous, and you find out that nothing bad happens, you learn that these situations are okay and you do not need to avoid them. But if you do not confront them, you will continue to believe that these situations are dangerous and you will keep avoiding them; you never give yourself the chance to learn differently. Thus, in vivo exposure helps you to better tell the difference between situations that actually may be dangerous or high-risk from those that are okay. If you felt okay going to the grocery store alone before, then it is probably okay to do it now.

Third, many people with PTSD think that if they stay in the situation that makes them anxious, their anxiety will stay high forever or even get worse until they lose their mind. However, if you stay in the situation long enough, you will find that your anxiety will go down. This process is called habituation. As a result of this process, your symptoms will go down as well.

Fourth, confronting feared situations and getting over your fears will help your self-esteem and make you feel more competent, because you will know that you can cope better with your problems. You will start doing things that you used to like and that you stopped doing because of your PTSD, and you will begin to enjoy life and do more.

For all these reasons we ask you to systematically confront relatively safe situations that you are now avoiding, beginning with easier ones and working your way up toward harder ones. Of course we do not suggest that you expose yourself to unsafe situations. The goal is not to help you see dangerous situations as safe but to keep you from avoiding situations that are realistically safe. In order to help you stop avoiding situations and people that used to be fun or important, we are going to work together to make a list of situations that you have been avoiding since the trauma. Your therapist will also want to find out from you how much distress or discomfort these situations would cause you if you weren't avoiding them.

Case Example #1: In Vivo Exposure

Here is an example showing how in vivo exposure works.

> *A little boy was sitting on the beach with his mother when an unexpected, huge wave from the ocean washed over them. The child got very upset and cried that he wanted to go home. The next day when it was time to go to the beach, the little boy began crying and refused to go. He kept saying, "No, no. Water come to me." In order to help him get over his fear of the water, his mother took him for walks on the beach over the next few days. She would hold his hand and gradually helped him walk closer to the water's edge. By the end of the week the boy was able to walk into the water alone. With patience, practice, encouragement, and gradual exposure, his fear of the water decreased.*

Case Example #2: In Vivo Exposure

Here is another example that illustrates in vivo exposure.

A taxicab driver who lived in New York had a fear of driving across bridges. This fear created serious problems with his work, since he was unable to drive people across bridges. Each time he was about to cross a bridge, he pretended that something was wrong with the taxi and called another cab to take his passengers. The taxicab driver, with the help of a therapist, practiced driving over bridges every day. Within a week, he was able to go across the bridge with the therapist following him in another car. By the end of 2 weeks, with repeated practice, he was able to drive over small bridges by himself.

Hopefully these examples help you understand that confronting the things you are scared of in a careful and systematic way can help you get over your fear. Because you have experienced a traumatic event, you may need more time to confront fears related to your experience. But with time, practice, and courage you will be able to confront the things that now make you afraid.

Some people tell us that they have been confronting situations but haven't gotten any better. It is important to know the difference between occasional, brief exposure and deliberate, systematic, repeated, prolonged exposure to feared situations. Confronting your fears in a careful and systematic way as we describe is what helps you get over them. Confronting a situation once for a short period and getting out of there while you are still very afraid doesn't give you a chance to learn that the situation is not dangerous and that anxiety does not remain forever. If you feel you have tried to confront these fears but haven't gotten any better in the past, please talk about this with your therapist so together you can figure out what went wrong and how to do it differently this time. We want you to engage in *therapeutic* exposure. An exposure that still leaves you scared is not therapeutic. An exposure that helps you decrease your fear, like the little boy at the ocean or the taxi driver in the examples above, is therapeutic. You and your therapist will come up with a list of therapeutic exposures for you to practice.

Introduction to SUDS

In order to find out how much discomfort or anxiety certain situations cause you, you and your therapist will use a SUDS scale. This 0–100 scale stands for *Subjective Units of Discomfort*. A SUDS rating of 100 indicates that you are very upset, the most you have ever been in your life, and 0 indicates no discomfort at all. Usually when people say they have a SUDS level of 100, they may be experiencing physical reactions, such as sweaty palms, heart palpitations, difficulty breathing, feelings of dizziness, and intense anxiety. So a rating of 100 is really extreme. But because people are different, a situation that makes one person feel a SUDS level of 100 may not be that bad for someone else. This is why we call it a subjective scale. For example, imagine that you and a friend are standing near a deep pool, and someone pushes you both in the water. If your friend cannot swim, she may feel a SUDS level of 100. But if you can swim, or are not afraid of deep water, you may feel a level of zero.

In order to make this SUDS scale fit you and your fears, you and your therapist will need to find out which situations represent different levels on the scale. Someone else's example may help:

0 = Watching TV in bed, very relaxed

25 = Taking a bus across town

50 = Making a mistake and being asked to meet her boss and explain the mistake

75 = Getting a phone call from her child's teacher

100 = Feeling like she felt during the worse moment of the trauma

You and your therapist are going to be using SUDS ratings to monitor your feelings during the imaginal and in vivo exposures.

In Vivo Exposure Hierarchy Construction

Your therapist will ask you for specific examples of situations, people, and places that you avoid because of your traumatic experience.

You and your therapist will record some of the situations you avoid and rate them on the SUDS scale in the session. You will be asked to take this list home with you and add to it any other situations you think of, and also rate how much anxiety and distress you think you will feel in these situations using the SUDS scale.

It is important that the situations are easily available to you so you can do them over and over. Situations that require a 3-hour drive each way are unrealistic for repeated practice. The situations should also be specific rather than general. For example, "going into a crowded street" or "going to a supermarket" are not specific enough. It is important to say a specific street or a specific supermarket, and at a specific time, because different streets and supermarkets and different times of the day may lead to different levels of anxiety. Also, going to the supermarket with a friend may be easier than going alone.

There are three main types of situations that are often avoided by people with PTSD:

1. First are situations that you think are dangerous, not because they are really dangerous but because you now see the world as a dangerous place. Situations of this type may include walking alone in safe areas after dark, going to a party, going to crowded places, driving along a highway, and being in parking lots.

2. Second are situations that are reminders of the traumatic event, such as wearing the same or similar clothing as you were wearing at the time the trauma occurred, smelling odors or hearing music that were there during the incident, and riding in a similar car. These types of situations are avoided not because you see them as dangerous but because they trigger memories of the traumatic event and cause you to feel bad. These are often realistically safe situations, even though they may make you feel uncomfortable or upset.

3. The third type of situation includes things like being involved in sports, clubs, hobbies, and friendships; wearing makeup and dressing nicely; going to church or synagogue or meetings; visiting friends or inviting people to your home for a meal; and generally doing other activities that you used to enjoy but have stopped doing since the trauma. Practicing these is very helpful for people who are depressed or who avoid situations and activities because they lost interest in them after the trauma.

To create your hierarchy, you will make a list of all the situations that you avoid or that make you feel uncomfortable using the In Vivo Exposure Hierarchy provided.

In Vivo Exposure Hierarchy

Name: _____

Date: _____

Therapist: _____

SUDS Anchor Points

0—— _____

50—— _____

100—— _____

Item	SUDS (Sess. 2)	SUDS (Final Sess.)
1. _____	_____	_____
2. _____	_____	_____
3. _____	_____	_____
4 _____	_____	_____
5. _____	_____	_____
6. _____	_____	_____
7. _____	_____	_____
8. _____	_____	_____
9. _____	_____	_____
10. _____	_____	_____
11. _____	_____	_____
12. _____	_____	_____
13. _____	_____	_____
14. _____	_____	_____
15. _____	_____	_____
16. _____	_____	_____
17. _____	_____	_____
18. _____	_____	_____

Some typical examples of upsetting situations for trauma survivors that usually lead to avoidance include:

1. In cases of assault, being around men you don't know, especially those who somehow remind you of the assailant (e.g., a man of the same race)

2. Someone standing close or coming up suddenly

3. Being touched by someone (especially someone unfamiliar)

4. Doing something similar to the trauma situation (e.g., for motor vehicle accident survivors, driving or riding in a car)

5. Walking down a street or being out in the open

6. Being alone at home (day or night)

7. Going somewhere alone at night

8. Being in a crowded mall or store

9. Talking to strangers

10. Driving a car or being stopped at a stoplight

11. Being in a parking lot

12. Riding in elevators or being in small, confined spaces

13. Reading about a similar event in the newspaper or hearing about it on television

14. Talking with someone about the trauma

15. Watching movies that remind you of the trauma (e.g., combat films, assault scenes)

16. Going to the area of town where the traumatic event happened

17. Riding public transportation

18. Hugging and kissing significant others

19. Sexual or physical contact

20. Listening to a song that you heard during the traumatic event or that was from that same time

21. Watching the news on TV

22. Wearing makeup or looking attractive

23. Going to a movie that has some violence

24. Taking an exercise class

25. Driving a car with unknown people and piles of unidentifiable material next to the road that you fear could be explosives

26. Coming upon a stopped car while driving and not being able to get around it

27. Smelling food or spices similar to those present during the traumatic experience

Safety Considerations When Constructing the In Vivo Exposure Hierarchy

It is important that the situations you plan to confront during in vivo exposure are safe or low-risk. We do not want you to put situations that are dangerous or high-risk on your list. For example, we would not want you to walk alone in areas where drugs are sold or in a park where crimes are regularly committed. Instead, we want you to pick situations that trigger your anxiety but are realistically safe. For example, you could walk in a public park with another person, or plan to walk alone in a safe area of the city.

In Vivo Assignments

In vivo exposure will begin with situations that make you a bit anxious but feel manageable (e.g., SUDS = 40 or 50), and then you will gradually progress up to the more upsetting situations (e.g., SUDS = 100). During the in vivo exposure exercise, you should plan to stay in the situation until your anxiety has a chance to go up (if it does) and then decrease significantly. We don't want you or your body to feel relief when you *leave* a situation that you are practicing for exposure. Details of the situations like time of day and the people that are around can be adjusted to get the level of anxiety during exposure that you are aiming for. For example, for Martha, going to the mall with her mother was SUDS of 60, while going alone was SUDS of 85. Although the time it takes to successfully complete an in vivo exposure will vary from situation to situation or person to person, in general, you may need to allow for 30 to 60 minutes of exposure time.

Please refer to the Model of Gradual In Vivo Exposure provided in the following section to help you with your in vivo exposures.

Model of Gradual In Vivo Exposure

Directions

Use this example to help you design your in vivo exposure assignments. It is important for you to stay in the situation for a long enough period of time that your anxiety can rise and then fall, or until there is a 50% decrease in your peak SUDS (Subjective Units of Discomfort, where 0 = no discomfort and 100 = panic-level discomfort). Write down your SUDS before and after the exposure using the In Vivo Exposure Homework Recording Form provided on page 41.

Example: Going to a Shopping Mall

1. "Coach" (a supportive friend or family member) goes with you to shopping mall and you walk around the mall together.

2. Coach goes with you to shopping mall and stays in a specific area of the mall while you walk around alone.

3. Coach goes with you to shopping mall and stays in a specific area while you walk into some stores alone.

4. Coach drives you to shopping mall and stays in parking lot while you walk around mall alone.

5. Coach drives you to shopping mall and leaves parking lot for an hour while you walk around mall alone.

6. You go to shopping mall alone and coach waits by a telephone in his or her home.

7. You go to shopping mall alone and don't tell coach.

In Vivo Exposure Homework

We want to make sure that you remember that the goal of in vivo exposure is to help you to be able to be in and stay in situations that remind you of the trauma without having high anxiety that interferes with your life. This part of the program involves having you confront situations that make you feel anxiety and a need to avoid. For it to work, you'll have to do a lot of exposure exercises, for a long period each time. It takes effort, time, and commitment, but it can produce excellent results.

You and your therapist will go over your In Vivo Exposure Hierarchy and decide which situations you will confront for homework. It is best to have two or more situations for homework. You should start with situations that you rated between 40 and 50 on the SUDS scale. By the end of treatment, you should have practiced all the situations listed on your hierarchy over and over.

When you are first practicing a situation, you may feel anxiety symptoms, such as your heart beating rapidly, your palms sweating, and feeling faint, and you may want to leave the situation immediately. But in order to overcome your fear, it is important that you stay in the situation until your anxiety decreases and that you realize that what you were afraid could happen (e.g., being attacked or "falling apart") did not actually happen. Once your anxiety has decreased a good deal, or by at least 50%, then you can stop the exposure and go on with other activities. However, if you leave the situation when you are still very anxious, you are again telling yourself that the situation is dangerous, that your anxiety remains forever, or that something terrible is going to happen to you. And the next time you go into that situation, your level of anxiety will be high again.

On the other hand, if you stay in the situation and realize that you are not really in danger, your anxiety will decrease, and eventually you will be able to go into it without fear. The more often you practice each situation on your list, the faster you will reach the point in which you will stop being anxious in those situations. You will go over the In Vivo Exposure Homework Recording Form with your therapist. You will use this form to rate your SUDS level before and after the exposure, as well as the peak, or highest, SUDS level. You will be asked to rate your SUDS level on many occasions throughout the course of your treatment. You may photocopy the In Vivo Exposure Homework Recording Form or download multiple copies from the Treatments *ThatWork*™ Web site (http://www.oup.com/us/ttw). We have also provided two sample completed forms on pp. 42 and 43 for you to use as models (figures 4.1 and 4.2).

Homework

Please use the Homework: Session 2 form provided at the end of this chapter to track your homework assignments.

✎ Continue breathing practice.

✎ Read about the common reactions to trauma several times a week; you may share this information with significant others.

✎ Review the list of avoided situations at home and add your own.

✎ Review the Model for Gradual In Vivo Exposure.

✎ Begin conducting in vivo exposure exercises.

✎ Listen to audiotape of entire session once.

In Vivo Exposure Homework Recording Form

Name: _____ Date: _____

1) Situation that you practiced _____

Date & Time	SUDS			Date & Time	SUDS		
	Pre	Post	Peak		Pre	Post	Peak
1.				5.			
2.				6.			
3.				7.			
4.				8.			

2) Situation that you practiced _____

Date & Time	SUDS			Date & Time	SUDS		
	Pre	Post	Peak		Pre	Post	Peak
1.				5.			
2.				6.			
3.				7.			
4.				8.			

3) Situation that you practiced _____

Date & Time	SUDS			Date & Time	SUDS		
	Pre	Post	Peak		Pre	Post	Peak
1.				5.			
2.				6.			
3.				7.			
4.				8.			

Client Name: _Mr. B_   Date: _8/2/05_

1) Situation that you practiced _walking around the army base for a couple of hours_

Date & Time	SUDS			Date & Time	SUDS		
	Pre	Post	Peak		Pre	Post	Peak
1. 8/3/05 4pm	80	75	85	5.			
2. 8/4/05 10am	30	20	60	6.			
3. 8/8/05 3pm	50	50	70	7.			
4. 8/9/05 4pm	40	25	55	8.			

On 8/4/06, I went to base with my wife instead of alone — it was easier that day

2) Situation that you practiced _watching the evening news — hearing about war_

Date & Time	SUDS			Date & Time	SUDS		
	Pre	Post	Peak		Pre	Post	Peak
1. 8/4/05 6pm	50	60	75	5. 8/8/05 6pm	35	35	50
2. 8/5/05 6pm	55	45	60	6. 8/9/05 6pm	40	35	55
3. 8/6/05 6pm	35	50	55	7.			
4. 8/7/05 6pm	40	40	60	8.			

3) Situation that you practiced _attending PTSD group at VA and talking in meeting_

Date & Time	SUDS			Date & Time	SUDS		
	Pre	Post	Peak		Pre	Post	Peak
1. 8/10/05	90	40	90	5.			
2. 8/17/05	80	30	80	6.			
3.				7.			
4.				8.			

Figure 4.1

Example of completed In Vivo Exposure Homework Recording Form for combat veteran

Clients Name: Ms. S _____ Date: 2/15/06 _____

1) Situation that you practiced _walking dog in the park_ _____

Date & Time	SUDS			Date & Time	SUDS		
	Pre	Post	Peak		Pre	Post	Peak
1. 2/22/06 1pm	60	40	80	5. 2/26/06 2pm	30	30	40
2. 2/23/06 2pm	55	40	60	6. 2/28/06 3pm	30	20	35
3. 2/24/06 6pm	70	50	70	7.			
4. 2/25/06 1pm	40	30	50	8.			

2) Situation that you practiced _going to a movie_ _____

Date & Time	SUDS			Date & Time	SUDS		
	Pre	Post	Peak		Pre	Post	Peak
1. 2/25/06 4pm	50	30	75	5.			
2. 2/28/06 7pm	40	30	55	6.			
3.				7.			
4.				8.			

3) Situation that you practiced _talking to male coworker in the lunchroom_ _____

Date & Time	SUDS			Date & Time	SUDS		
	Pre	Post	Peak		Pre	Post	Peak
1. 2/22/06 12pm	75	75	90	5.			
2. 2/24/06 12pm	75	60	80	6.			
3. 2/27/06 10am	60	45	60	7.			
4.				8.			

Note — the last time I did this, I sat and talked to a guy for over 1 hour, and definitely felt my nervousness get better, but was still worried that he'd ask me out or something.

Figure 4.2

Example of completed In Vivo Exposure Homework Recording Form for rape survivor

Homework: Session 2

Name: _____ Date: _____

Therapist: _____

1. Continue breathing practice.

2. Read Common Reactions to Trauma information several times a week; share with important people in your life.

3. Review the list of avoided situations at home and add additional situations.

4. Begin in vivo assignments. Use the In Vivo Exposure Homework Recording Form to fill in SUDS levels before and after the exposure, as well as your peak SUDS level. Remember to stay in the situation long enough for your anxiety to come down.

_____

_____

_____

_____

5. Listen to audiotape of entire session at least once.

Chapter 5   *Session 3*

Goals

- To review homework

- To discuss the rationale for imaginal exposure with your therapist

- To do your first imaginal exposure to the trauma memory

Imaginal Exposure

Imaginal exposure, or revisiting the trauma memory in your imagination, is a procedure in which you will be asked to go over the traumatic event while saying it out loud, in the present tense. It is meant to:

- Help you get in touch with all of the important aspects of the trauma memory: what actually happened, what you were thinking, what you were feeling, and what bodily sensations you had.

- Help you get in touch with your emotions about the traumatic event.

- Help you talk about the memory in your own words at your own pace.

Prolonged or Multiple Incident Traumas

For people with a traumatic event that lasted many hours or days or longer (e.g., a period of several days of captivity) or multiple incident traumas (e.g., repeated assaults, recurring childhood sexual abuse, multiple incidents of combat), you will need to decide with your therapist which of the traumatic memories you will work on first. Typically, these are the memories that bother you most right now. In most cases, working on the most disturbing memory first will help you get over less upsetting memories.

It is important to remember that even if you feel temporarily more upset after some exposure sessions, especially the early ones, this just means that you are beginning to emotionally process these memories. You are beginning to heal from the trauma. If you are worried about how you will react, especially during the early sessions of imaginal exposure, it is fine to bring a supportive person with you to wait and drive home with you afterward.

Rationale for Imaginal Exposure

You and your therapist will spend most of session 3 helping you revisit and recount aloud the memory of your trauma. It is not easy to understand and make sense of traumatic experiences. When you think about the incident or are reminded of it, you may experience extreme anxiety and other bad feelings. The trauma was a very frightening and upsetting experience, so you tend to push away or avoid the painful memories. You may tell yourself not to think about it or that you just have to forget it. Other people often advise you to do the same. Also, your friends, family, and partner may feel uncomfortable hearing about the trauma, and this may influence you not to talk about it. But, as you have already discovered, no matter how hard you try to push away thoughts about the trauma, the experience comes back to haunt you through distressing thoughts and feelings, nightmares, and flashbacks. We view these reexperiencing symptoms as a sign that the trauma is still "unfinished business."

In this treatment our goal is to help you to process the memories connected with the trauma by having you remember them for an extended period. Staying with these memories, rather than running away from them, will help you process and digest the memory and put it in the past. You will learn that remembering the trauma, although painful and unpleasant, is not dangerous. This will also decrease the anxiety and fear that are linked with the memory. It is natural to want to avoid painful experiences such as memories, feelings, and situations that remind you of the trauma. However, the more you avoid dealing with the memories, the more they disturb your life. Our aim is to have you control the memories, instead of having the memories control you.

In order to explain to you why it is so difficult yet important to process the traumatic memory, let's look at an example:

Suppose you have eaten a very large and heavy meal (or spoiled food) and now you have a stomachache, nausea, etc. These will stay until you have digested the food, but afterward, you will feel great relief. Flashbacks, nightmares, and troublesome thoughts continue to occur because you have not digested the traumatic memory. Today you are going to start digesting or processing your heavy memories so that they will stop interfering with your daily life.

Another way to explain why it is so difficult to digest and process a traumatic memory is by the following example:

Imagine that your memory is like a big file cabinet. Past experiences are each filed into a proper drawer. In this way you organize your experiences and make sense of them. For example, you have a file for restaurant experiences. Every time you go to eat in a restaurant, you open the restaurant file and you know what will happen. This is the way in which you remember how to behave in a restaurant and what to expect. But traumatic events do not have a file. This is because unlike the restaurant experience, where you know exactly what will happen (you will be seated, given a menu, you will choose your food, get a check, and pay), traumas are unpredictable. Even if you have had several traffic accidents in which you were not injured, you never know how the next accident will end. In this way each trauma is unique and therefore needs much more effort to process. Part of recovering from a traumatic experience is being able to organize the traumatic memory and file it in long-term memory so you can move on with the business of your life.

One more example, which is very helpful if you already think about the trauma all the time and can't understand how imaginal exposure will be different or useful:

Imagine that your traumatic event is recorded in your brain like a book, with paragraphs, pages, and chapters. It is a book that has a story with a beginning, middle, and end. Because you have tried to avoid thinking about your trauma since it occurred, you have never read the book from the beginning to the end. Whenever you have a flashback, the book is opened to the paragraph where the flashback is written, and opening the book is painful and distressing. So you say to yourself, "I don't like this book," and you try hard to close it. The same thing happens when you have the next flashback or thought about your trauma. And this is why you have not read what is written in the book. In imaginal exposure, we will read the book together from the beginning to the end. This will give you an opportunity to view the traumatic event and its meaning from your perspective today, knowing you made it out okay, rather than from the perspective of the past when the trauma happened, when it was still terrifying. In this way, we will help you to make sense of a terrible experience that happened to you.

So the goal of imaginal exposure is to enable you to have thoughts about the trauma, to talk about it, or to see triggers of it without getting so upset or anxious that it disrupts your life. It will always be a bad memory of something that should never have happened, but it doesn't have to be so painful. This part of the program involves having you confront trauma-related memories that generate both anxiety and an urge to avoid. For it to work, you will do it over and over, for a long period each time.

So there are several ways in which imaginal exposure will help you recover from your PTSD. Repeated revisiting and recounting of the trauma memories will:

1. Help you process and organize your traumatic memory and see it from the point of view of the present rather than from the point of view of the past when the trauma occurred.

2. Help you understand the difference between "remembering" the traumatic event and having it happen again. Many people tell us that when they think about the trauma they feel as if it is happening again, so it is no wonder that they are so anxious and upset when they think about the trauma. Fear is an emotion we have when we feel in danger. However, remembering a trauma that happened in the past is not dangerous. Going over the traumatic memory again and again helps strengthen this difference between the present (remembering) and the past (being traumatized) so that remembering the trauma does not make you so anxious and distressed.

3. Lower your anxiety. We call this habituation. When this happens, you learn that anxiety does not last "forever" if you stay in the memory rather than pushing it away. Generally, the more you confront the trauma memory, the faster you will habituate.

4. Help you see the difference between the specific trauma and similar but safe situations. For example, a rape victim may spread her fear of the assailant to men that remind her of the assailant. Repeatedly imaging the particular assailant (e.g., his blue eyes) will help her see the difference between that man and all other men, hopefully reducing the fear of men in general.

5. Help you to feel more in control and more competent. You will feel better about yourself as you stop avoiding and instead master your fears. You will learn that you can remember the trauma if you want to and put it aside if you don't want to think about it. You also learn that you can be anxious and do it anyway.

Conducting Imaginal Exposure

Your therapist will ask you to recall the memories of the trauma. It's best to start at a point in the memory that is a little bit before the trauma actually occurred, so that you have a chance to enter the image and get connected to it. So you may want to begin your story at a point that is at least several minutes before the situation got bad or frightening. You will then go on through the story of the trauma, up until the danger is over or you are out of the situation.

It is best for you to close your eyes while you do this so you won't be distracted and can picture it in your mind's eye. Your therapist will ask you to recall these painful memories as vividly as possible and to picture them in your mind's eye. We call this revisiting the trauma memory. Your therapist will ask you to describe the experience in the present tense, as if it were happening now, right here. You will recount aloud what happened during the trauma in as much detail as you can manage. You and your therapist will work on this together. If you start to feel uncomfortable and want to run away or avoid it by leaving the image, your therapist will help you to stay with it. From time to time, while you are revisiting the trauma, your therapist will ask you for your anxiety level on the 0–100 SUDS scale. Please just try to answer quickly with the first number that comes to mind to describe how you feel right then, not how you felt at that point in the trauma. Because it is important that you stay in the imaginal exposure for a lengthy period of time, when you finish recounting the trauma, your therapist will ask you to start all over again, without pause. You may do this several times within one session; the number of times depends on how long it takes you to go through the memory. It's important that you do not push the memories away, even if they are painful. Remember, memories are not dangerous, even if they feel bad. Your therapist will not say much in response to you until your imaginal exposure is done, but you'll have time afterward to talk about your experience with it.

After the imaginal exposure to your trauma memory you will have many emotions and thoughts. Therefore, it is important to begin processing this experience with your therapist. Your therapist will ask you to describe your thoughts and feelings about the imaginal exposure and to pay attention to what happened with your anxiety. Does it get any easier for you to talk about what happened? Do you start to think about things any differently? Even if it doesn't seem to be getting any easier yet, you should be proud that you are sticking with it and allowing yourself to face these painful memories. That is probably a big change for you. You and your therapist will also talk about any important thoughts or beliefs that come up for you. Sometimes people will see things differently after going through the memory over and over. For example, many people realize that they could not have prevented the traumatic experience, or that it wasn't their fault, or that they did the best they could. You and your therapist will also talk about any ideas that come out during exposure, such as blaming yourself, or not trusting people. Some questions to consider when looking at your thoughts about the trauma:

- When did you start viewing it this way? What makes you think this way?

- How do you feel when you think of it in this way?

- What would you tell your daughter/sister/friend if she were thinking this way?

- What would you tell your son/brother/friend if he had been through a similar experience?

- What does it mean to you that this happened to you?

- What does it say about you?

- Why do you think you currently have PTSD?

- How does it fit with what you've learned about common reactions to trauma?

We have found that sometimes people are scared to express their feelings. Some people are afraid to cry because they think they will never stop. You may feel that you need to maintain control, and then you may do things that interfere with processing the memory. For example, some people try to avoid picturing very scary parts of their memories, such as the image of an oncoming car just before the crash, an assailant's face, or being threatened with a weapon. It is good for you to remember that you are safe in the therapy room with your therapist and that what you are revisiting is a memory and is not happening now.

Words of Encouragement

We know that confronting your fears can be hard in the beginning. If it weren't, you wouldn't need to seek this treatment. It takes courage, and we don't use that word loosely. Courage is being scared and doing it anyway. But we know it is worth it. We have seen so many people go through this program or similar programs and feel like they finally can get back on track and get on with their lives that we know it is worth it. Your work here will pay off for the rest of your life. You will notice the difference, and your family and friends will notice the difference. But it can be hard in the beginning—going through the memory of what happened and staying with it and the feelings and then doing it over and over again. What helps is the knowledge that it will get easier. You've made the decision that you need help, so take it. Use this chance and make the most of it. We know you won't be sorry. Good luck! You're worth it!

Homework

Please use the Homework: Sessions 3–10 form provided at the end of this chapter to track your homework assignments over the remaining sessions.

✎ Listen to the tape of imaginal exposure once a day. Note: you should not listen to the exposure tape before you go to sleep, because we don't want to interfere with your sleep. Also, you should not let others listen to the tape because we don't want you to have to deal with other people's reactions to it while you are trying to sort out your own reactions and feelings about it. And if you are letting other people listen to your tapes, you may leave out something important because you are worried how someone else would react to it.

✎ Record your reactions to the imaginal exposure using the Imaginal Exposure Homework Recording Form provided at the end of this chapter. You may photocopy this form or download multiple copies at the Treatments *That Work*™ Web site at www.oup.com/us/ttw. We have also provided two sample completed forms below and on p. 53 for you to use as models (figures 5.1 and 5.2).

✎ Continue with in vivo exposure exercises daily, working up the hierarchy with SUDS levels and writing down when you practice on the In Vivo Exposure Homework Recording Form (see chapter 4). If you don't have your sheets with you and you do an in vivo exposure, you can write down your SUDS and the situation, date, and time on any paper and then transfer it to this sheet when you get back to it.

✎ Listen to audiotape of entire session once.

Client Name: _Mr. B_   Date: _9/8/05_

Instructions: Please record your SUDS ratings on a 0–100 scale (where 0 = no discomfort and 100 = maximal discomfort, anxiety, and panic) before and after you listen to the audiotape of the imaginal exposure.

Tape #: _7 (fourth exposure — hot spots)_

DATE & TIME	3/2/06 7pm	3/3/06 5pm	3/4/06 4pm	3/5/06 10am
SUDS Pre	50	50	40	30
SUDS Post	40	30	35	30
Peak SUDS	50	55	40	50

DATE & TIME	3/7/06 7pm	3/8/06 6pm		
SUDS Pre	30	30		
SUDS Post	20	20		
Peak SUDS	50	35		

Figure 5.1

Example of completed Imaginal Exposure Homework Recording Form for combat veteran

Client Name: Ms. S   Date: 3/1/06

Instructions: Please record your SUDS ratings on a 0–100 scale (where 0 = no discomfort and 100 = maximal discomfort, anxiety, and panic) before and after you listen to the audiotape of the imaginal exposure.

Tape #: 1 (first exposure)

DATE & TIME	3/2/06 7pm	3/3/06 5pm	3/4/06 4pm	3/5/06 10am
SUDS Pre	80	80	70	40
SUDS Post	70	70	50	60
Peak SUDS	90	80	75	65

DATE & TIME	3/7/06 7pm	3/8/06 6pm		
SUDS Pre	50	40		
SUDS Post	40	30		
Peak SUDS	60	40		

Figure 5.2

Example of completed Imaginal Exposure Homework Recording Form for rape survivor

Imaginal Exposure Homework Recording Form

Name: _____ Date: _____

Instructions: Please record your SUDS ratings on a 0–100 scale (where 0 = no discomfort and 100 = maximal discomfort, anxiety, and panic) before and after you listen to the audiotape of the imaginal exposure.

Tape #: _____

DATE & TIME				
SUDS Pre				
SUDS Post				
Peak SUDS				

DATE & TIME				
SUDS Pre				
SUDS Post				
Peak SUDS				

Homework: Sessions 3–10

Name: _____ Date: _____

Therapist: _____ Session: _____

1. Continue breathing practice.

2. Listen to audiotape of imaginal exposure at least once a day, using the Imaginal Exposure Homework Recording Form, and rate your SUDS.

3. Continue with in vivo exposure exercises daily, working up the hierarchy with SUDS levels:

_____

_____

_____

_____

4. Listen to audiotape of session one time.

Chapter 6　　*Anticipating and Solving Problems*

Goals

- ▨ To learn about common problems that may interfere with treatment

- ▨ To learn ways of working through problems and difficulties

Even with all of our experience working with survivors of trauma and using this treatment, and even with all the hard work of you and your therapist, sometimes it is difficult for people to get all they can out of PE. At this point in treatment, you have some sense of how you are responding and whether you are having any difficulties that might interfere with getting all that you want out of this program. Common problems that get in the way of treatment and your improvement include avoidance (our old friend, remember?); not being connected enough to your emotions (under-engaged) or being connected *too much* (over-engaged) during revisiting and recounting your traumatic memories; not tolerating your emotional distress; and *persistently feeling* other negative emotions, such as anger. Fortunately, if you and your therapist are aware of what's happening, there are some things you both can do to help.

Importance of the Treatment Model

Emotional Processing Theory (PE) was described in chapter 1 of this workbook. It is important to keep this theory in mind when trying to solve problems and design the best therapy program for you.

For example, a good in vivo exposure hierarchy is made up of situations that match your specific fears: that is, they make you feel fearful or distressed. Are the in vivo exercises right for you? Do they matter to you? Are they hitting the nail on the head of your fear or are you indifferent to them? Perhaps they don't distress you? Keeping the theory in mind always helps when trying to plan and modify treatment. For example, a client who always gives a very quick account of her trauma memory during imaginal exposures, and works hard to keep her feelings shut down while doing so, is most likely not bringing to mind all of the important pieces of her fear structure—she is avoiding the feelings, thoughts, or images that are associated with her trauma memory. If this happens to you, you need to remember why this avoidance, although understandable, interferes with your recovery from PTSD, and work to find ways to increase your engagement with all the aspects of your trauma memory so that you can process it.

Implementing Effective In Vivo and Imaginal Exposure

Modifying In Vivo Exposure

In session 2, you and your therapist created a list of situations, places, people, or activities that you fear and avoid (or suffer through if necessary, but as briefly as possible). Typically, people systematically move up the hierarchy, practicing each situation repeatedly until the anxiety or distress goes down and the person no longer sees the situation as dangerous or difficult.

People with PTSD almost always struggle with avoidance during treatment. The urges to avoid are understandable, but as we've discussed repeatedly, avoidance maintains the trauma-related fear and anxiety. If you are struggling with doing your in vivo exposures, it is often useful to change your hierarchy by breaking each situation into smaller steps. If it becomes clear that an in vivo exposure situation is too hard to confront at the present time, find ways to make it less difficult or to reduce your SUDS level. Sometimes having a friend or family member accompany you during the exposure exercise helps you manage your distress (as in the example you saw in chapter 4 of a woman progressing up through her in vivo exposure of going to the mall). Changing other factors like time of day or location of the exposure may also decrease the distress associated with the exercise and make it easier to do. When you have mastered the modified (easier) exposure situation, you can move on to the one that you could not confront and then to more difficult situations.

Occasionally, as treatment progresses, a person may not experience a reduction in fear despite what appears to be good and repeated exposure. In these cases, it is helpful to look closely at what you are actually *doing* during the in vivo exposure exercises. Think about exactly how you are carrying out the exposure, how long it lasts, and when you end it. Do you stay in the situation long enough to allow your fear to decrease? Or are you escaping the situation while still very anxious? Look also for subtle avoidance and "safety behaviors" (e.g., being only with "safe" people, shopping only when the stores are less crowded, always choosing a female clerk or cashier to deal with, etc.) that may interfere with fear reduction by preventing you from realizing that the situations are not dangerous even when you do not do your safety behaviors.

Finally, look for avoidance that you might not even be aware of. One client puzzled us because, although consistently doing her exposure homework between sessions, she was not habituating at all, and at midtreatment, her PTSD symptoms were higher than they were at pretreatment. When the therapist tried to understand this lack of progress by discussing it with the client, it became evident that the client was trying to keep herself emotionally detached while doing her homework. Also, whenever she wasn't actually doing her exposure homework, she was completely avoiding all trauma-related triggers, thoughts, and feelings. She and her therapist hadn't been aware of the extent of her avoidance. The therapist helped the client see how her avoidance was interfering with her treatment, and the client began to recognize and reduce her extensive avoidance behavior in daily life. As a result, her PTSD symptoms quickly began to improve. Another client reported doing her exposures as instructed, spending more time out and alone at night, without apparent benefit. When asked for details, it turned out she was preparing her keys in her hand before she raced from her car to the front door and could almost not get the door unlocked fast enough. When she quickly slammed the door, she felt as if she had narrowly escaped danger. We had to explain how conducting exposure in this manner was not *therapeutic;* it was important to let her mind and body learn that she had nothing to fear from the dark outside her front door.

Modifying Imaginal Exposure

In PE, imaginal exposure, or revisiting and recounting the trauma memories, is conducted in such a way to get you emotionally engaged with the memory and with the feelings you get by facing the memory. Through repeatedly revisiting and recounting the trauma memory, the images, thoughts, and feelings that are associated with the memory are organized and integrated. In order to process and digest your traumatic experience, it is important to be emotionally connected with the memory and with the feelings triggered by it, but at the same time to not be overwhelmed with anxiety and to feel in control. The experience should help you learn that memories are not dangerous and that anxiety does not last forever.

It is common for PTSD sufferers to shut down their feelings when thinking or talking about a trauma. That is why the standard procedures for imaginal exposure are designed to encourage emotional engagement by asking you to keep your eyes closed, vividly imagine and visualize the traumatic scene as if it is happening now, use the present tense, and include the thoughts, emotions, physical sensations, and behaviors that you experienced during the traumatic event. The therapist prompts for details that are missing (i.e., "What are you feeling as this happens?" or "What are you thinking as he says that?") and monitors your distress level throughout the revisiting and recounting of the trauma memory. In our experience, the most frequent problem with emotional engagement is without doubt under-engagement, or keeping the emotions at arm's length. Much less frequently, the person becomes overwhelmed with emotions during imaginal exposure and feels a loss of control. We term this experience "over-engagement."

Under-Engagement

As used in PE, the term "under-engagement" refers to difficulty being in touch with the emotional aspects of the trauma memory. It is most commonly encountered in imaginal exposure but may also occur with in vivo exposure. In the case of revisiting and recounting the trauma memory, the person may describe her trauma, even in great detail, yet feel disconnected from it emotionally or not be able to visualize what happened. She may report feeling numb or detached. Distress or anxiety levels during the exposure are typically low when someone is under-engaged. However, the under-engaged person could also report high distress levels (SUDS) even when it doesn't look as though she is that upset. Sometimes the person who is under-engaged seems stilted or distant, as if she is reading a police report rather than giving a first-person account of a traumatic event.

You can work to allow yourself to become emotionally engaged first by following the standard procedures of keeping your eyes closed and using the present tense. These procedures promote emotional connection to the memory. Make sure you include as much detail as you can, including bodily sensations, feelings, and thoughts (e.g., describe what you see; describe the room; describe how it smells; describe what you are wearing, what you are feeling, what you are thinking, etc.).

It is important for you to remember that your memories are not dangerous, even though they are upsetting, and that recounting and visualizing the memory is not the same as reencountering the trauma and being traumatized again. Remember that being distressed is not dangerous. Our research findings show that being emotionally engaged with the traumatic memory helps recovery. Think about what you can do to help get around this wall you have built to protect yourself from your emotions. Unfortunately, there is no way to the other side of the pain except through it. Stick it out, let yourself experience everything you have to feel, and you can get to the other side. Protect yourself too much, and you may get stuck where you are.

Over-Engagement

As used in PE, the term "over-engagement" refers to excessive emotional distress elicited by imaginal exposure to the trauma memory or by in vivo exposure to trauma reminders. Imaginal confrontation with frightening memories or images is usually upsetting, and most people cry and become upset, especially in the early stage of PE. We want you to be able to learn from this experience that memories are not dangerous, even when they are painful, that you are not losing your mind, that you are not losing control, and that anxiety does not last indefinitely.

If this is a problem for you, and you become so emotionally upset during the revisiting and recounting of your trauma that you don't think you are learning that they are not dangerous, there are things that you and your therapist can do. Do you have difficulty maintaining a sense of being grounded and safe in the present moment? Does recounting the trauma memory feel to you as though you are actually reencountering the trauma? Are you having body memories or flashbacks during imaginal exposure? Are you able to respond to the therapist's questions or directions? Do you feel detached or dissociated from present experience? Does it feel completely like you are back there and it is happening rather than telling the story in the therapist's office? Do you feel stuck?

In modifying the imaginal exposure procedures, the primary goal is to help you to successfully describe some part of the trauma memory while managing your distress and staying grounded in the present, knowing that you are safe. It does not mean not feeling upset, but it does mean that you are able to learn that revisiting your traumatic memory is not dangerous and that you can think about your trauma in new ways.

A first step is to reverse or change the procedures that are designed to promote engagement: maybe keep your eyes open while describing the exposure scene, and use the past rather than present tense in narrating the trauma memory. Sometimes these two changes alone reduce engagement enough. It may be helpful to remind yourself that you made it through the trauma, and you can keep one foot grounded in your therapist's office and the other foot in the memory and the imaginal exposure.

An alternative procedure for people who are over-engaged is writing the trauma narrative instead of talking about it. This can be done in session and also as homework between sessions. If you try this, write down what happened, and include the thoughts, feelings, actions, and sensations as well as events of what happened. When done in session, as you are able to write the trauma narrative and begin to show signs of feeling more in control, you can then read the narrative out loud.

Other Obstacles to Successful Exposure

Avoidance

Confrontation with feared situations or stimuli always triggers urges to escape or avoid, so avoidance is the most commonly encountered problem for effective exposure both in and out of the therapist's office. The middle phase of treatment is often difficult for some people. This is sometimes the "feeling worse before you feel better" stage of therapy.

When you are really having a hard time with wanting to avoid, keep in mind that this is part of the PTSD and exactly why you went into treatment. If it were easy, you would have done it already. Remember that while avoidance reduces anxiety in the short term, in the long run it maintains fear and prevents you from learning that the avoided situations (or thoughts, memories, impulses, or images) are not harmful or dangerous.

As we mentioned above, you may need to take a close look at the in vivo exposure exercises and break them down into a more gradual progression.

We sometimes describe this struggle as sitting on a fence between exposure and avoidance. We know it is difficult to get off the fence, but sitting on it keeps the fear and slows progress. We encourage people to "*choose* to feel" anxiety in the service of mastery and recovery, rather than only having it triggered against one's will. A core aim is to learn that while anxiety is not comfortable, it is not dangerous, and that treatment involves learning to tolerate the anxiety triggered by exposures or by not avoiding.

Finally, it may be helpful to remember why you went for treatment in the first place (i.e., the ways in which your PTSD symptoms interfere with your life). Keep yourself motivated, even in the rough spots.

Anger and Other Negative Emotions

While exposure therapy was originally conceived as a treatment for the reduction of excessive or unrealistic anxiety, our experience over years of treating PTSD sufferers has taught us that PE facilitates the emotional processing of much more than fear and anxiety. Strong emotions are often stirred up and activated in the process of PE. People often report feelings of anger, rage, sadness, grief, shame, and guilt when revisiting the traumatic memory and at other points in processing their traumas. Of these, anger has probably had the most attention.

Although it is normal and justified to feel anger when thinking about your trauma, it is not good to get stuck in it. We have found that for many people it seems easier to feel anger than fear or sadness. Think about how angry you are and whether that is holding you back. Think about what you might need to do to get past that anger.

Remember that even though exposure therapy may not be for everyone, it has received stronger evidence in support of its efficacy in reducing PTSD than any other treatment and should be considered a first-line intervention unless ruled out for some reason. We feel strongly that even when problems come up, if possible, find a way to keep PE as the focus of your treatment. Reducing PTSD, depression, and related symptoms, as well as increasing your sense of confidence and self-efficacy, will help you to cope better now and in the future. We know it's tough, but we know it's worth the effort. Stick with it and do all you can to get the most out of this opportunity.

Chapter 7

Intermediate Sessions

(Session 4 to the end of treatment)

Goals

- To review homework

- To revisit and recount your traumatic memory using imaginal exposure

- Starting about session 5, you will focus on "hot spots" (the parts of the memory that are still causing the most distress and anxiety) more as therapy goes on.

- To discuss the experience of revisiting the trauma memory

- To discuss in vivo exposure

- To plan the next week's homework

Homework Review

By this point in therapy, we hope that you understand how confronting the memories of your trauma and safe situations that remind you of the trauma can help you get past what happened to you. We hope you are spending hours every day working on your homework, to help your processing along. You should be listening to the tape of the imaginal exposure every day. Don't just "listen" passively, but really connect to the imaginal exposure like you do in session with your therapist. You should practice the imaginal exposure in a quiet, private place where no one else can hear the tape playing. Your eyes should be closed during the duration of the exposure. Be sure you are in a place where you feel safe keeping your eyes closed for this long. Try to picture in your mind's eye what you are describing on the tape, letting yourself feel everything that it triggers and staying with the images and memories and feelings. You should give yourself a few minutes after the imaginal exposure to process the experience for yourself, thinking about how your reactions are changing and what you still need to work on. Is your anxiety getting less? Are you feeling angry? Are you feeling depressed? Are you still blaming yourself? Have you begun to let yourself off the hook and realize you did the best you could? Don't try to force how you think you "should" be thinking about it, but do stay open to allowing your thoughts and feelings about it to change. Don't be surprised if you find yourself feeling less distressed about things that have always been very disturbing to you. It doesn't mean that the occurrence of the trauma was not important, it means that the impact it has in your life NOW is lessening.

Are you putting as much effort as you could be into doing the in vivo exposure exercises? We know they are time consuming, but it is true that the more time you put into it, the more benefit you will get out of it. This treatment program is not very long, best described in weeks rather than months, so putting in as much effort as you can while you are going through it will pay off. Are you noticing the in vivo exposure exercises getting easier? You need to pat yourself on your back for all the work you are putting into this.

Imaginal Exposure

Starting at about session 4 or 5, when you and your therapist are working in the session on your revisiting the memory of what happened to you (imaginal exposure), your therapist will ask you to slow down during the recounting of your trauma and focus in more detail on what you are seeing, hearing, and feeling. You will still give your SUDS ratings every 5 minutes. As usual, you should just call out your rating as quickly as possible and don't leave the image. Just as before, you will close your eyes and try to vividly imagine what happened at the time of the trauma. Use the present tense, as if it were occurring now, and include what happened and what you were feeling and thinking as you went through this experience. At this point in your work, you should be including *all* details. If it is in your memory, please say it out loud. Don't worry about what it sounds like. You will continue imaginal exposure for 30–45 minutes without interruption, until your distress levels decrease. This can take a while. In fact, sometimes it takes several sessions of imaginal exposure before people begin to experience a decrease in distress levels or to "habituate." If this happens to you, the important thing to remember is that this does not mean you won't get better or won't benefit from the treatment. Our studies have shown that people get better at different rates and that not feeling better by the end of a session of imaginal exposure does not mean that you will have a worse outcome from therapy.

Are you having any difficulty letting go of your feelings during the imaginal exposure? Remember that you are safe in your therapist's office and that an important part of revisiting trauma memories is the connection to the feelings that are associated with them. Remind yourself that memories are not dangerous even if they make you feel upset or anxious. You are stronger than your memories.

As the therapy progresses (starting about session 5), it will be useful to focus on "hot spots" more and more. Hot spots are described in the next section.

Hot Spots

Up to this point, each time you have done your imaginal exposure, you have described the entire memory of what happened to you. And we hope that you have been making progress and have begun to experience the decrease in anxiety that we expect to see, at least with some of the relatively less disturbing parts of the memory. When you reach this point, you and your therapist are going to do the imaginal exposure a little differently.

When someone starts getting the benefit of habituation to some aspects of the trauma experience (as we said above, these are usually the relatively less distressing parts of the memory), we begin using a different procedure that helps to emotionally process the most difficult moments. You and your therapist will discuss, based on your last exposure and on your listening to the imaginal exposure tape for homework, what the most upsetting parts of this memory are for you now. And then starting in your next session (probably around session 5), rather than going through the entire memory from beginning to end, your therapist will ask you to focus the revisiting on each of these "hot spots," one at a time. You will pick one to begin with and you will repeat that one part of the memory over and over just by itself, focusing in closely and describing what happened in great detail, as if in slow motion, including what you felt, saw, heard, and thought. You will repeat it as many times as necessary to "wear it out" or allow a big decease in your SUDS level. When that part seems to have been sufficiently processed, you will move to the next one. It is similar to what sometimes happens during a massage when they work on a knot over and over until it is smoothed out. One of our patients said it was like listening to a record with skips and we worked on the skips so it didn't skip anymore and played all the way through smoothly. Another likened it to directly cleaning a wound that had caused infection in the entire body after antibiotic treatment had begun to work and make her feel better overall.

When your hot spot work is completed and you can visualize and describe all of these worst spots without much distress, you will return to focusing on and describing the entire trauma memory, putting it all back together. This should be done in the last session or two of treatment. Remember, one of the goals of PE is to have you emerge from the therapy with a well-organized and whole story of what happened to you, complete with the thoughts and feelings you had at the time.

For some people with more than one trauma or with a trauma that happened more than once (e.g., childhood sexual abuse or repeated incidents of combat), it may also be necessary to focus the imaginal exposure on several traumatic memories. We suggest that you do not move on to another trauma memory until you and your therapist have seen some progress with the first memory. Because we try to focus the initial revisiting on the "worst" trauma memory or the one that seems to be causing the most re-experiencing symptoms, the benefits of working through this memory often transfer to the other trauma memories so that they are not as bad when you start working on them. But if any other memories are still very upsetting, you may want to work on these as well. You and your therapist will discuss this and decide together whether or not it seems necessary.

Processing the Imaginal Exposure

As described in detail in session 3, you will process the imaginal exposure with your therapist after you have finished revisiting the trauma. This is where you will talk about the experience of revisiting and recounting the trauma memory, how you are thinking and feeling about the trauma, any changes you are noticing as you process the memories, and what meaning the trauma has in your life now. You will talk about how it has affected your life and how your thoughts about it may be changing. You will also talk about what you need to keep working on. Usually, as treatment progresses, people develop new perspectives on the trauma. These new perspectives are often more realistic, and the memory of the trauma becomes less likely to trigger strong feelings of distress or anxiety. Other negative emotions that are connected to the trauma—sadness, shame, anger, and guilt, for example—often decrease as well.

Although the goal of revisiting the trauma memory is not to recover forgotten memories, sometimes new material does emerge in the hot spot work as people identify the most terrifying moments of the traumatic incidents, e.g., "I thought the next time my parents would see me would be in a coffin," or "I was worried he would hit me in the eyes and blind me and then, even if I survived, I'd never be able to work again." It is important to focus the revisiting on these difficult moments, too, and to talk about them with your therapist.

In Vivo Exposure

You should continue your daily in vivo exposure homework assignments and should be moving up the in vivo hierarchy as treatment progresses. You should continue to practice each exposure item until it becomes easier, ideally until it produces only mild anxiety or discomfort. As your anxiety decreases and your confidence increases, we encourage you to do as much as you can to "take back" your life and to find ways to do in vivo exposure in day-to-day life.

Homework

✎ Continue breathing practice.

✎ Listen to the tape of that week's imaginal exposure once a day. Note: you should not listen to the exposure tape before you go to bed, because we don't want to interfere with your sleep. Also, you should not let others listen to the tape because we don't want you to complicate your recovery by having to deal with other people's reactions while sorting out your own. And if you are allowing other people to listen to your tapes, you may leave out important parts of your story because you are worried about how someone else would react to it. Finally, each week, we would rather you listen to the imaginal exposure from the session you most recently had, and not go back and listen to the earlier sessions of the trauma recounting. This is because as your therapy progresses, the way that you describe and think and feel about your trauma will likely shift and change. It's important that you move forward as your trauma processing moves forward.

✎ Record your reactions to the imaginal exposure using the Imaginal Exposure Homework Recording Form (see p. 54).

✎ Continue with in vivo exposure exercises daily, working up the hierarchy with SUDS levels and recording your practices on the In Vivo Exposure Homework Recording Form (see p. 41).

✎ Listen to audiotape of each session once.

Chapter 8

Final Session

Goals

- ■ To continue revisiting and recounting your trauma via imaginal exposure

- ■ To review your progress in treatment with your therapist and discuss continued practice

- ■ To wrap up your therapy

Imaginal Exposure

In this last session, you will spend about 20–30 minutes in imaginal exposure. You will go through the entire trauma memory in this session, rather than working on hot spots. It is important to go through the beginning, middle, and end of your story. At this point in your therapy, it is likely that the way you're thinking and feeling about the trauma has changed, and your story will reflect this. When you finish the imaginal exposure, you will talk about the experience ("processing") as you have done before. However, in this discussion, it is helpful for you and your therapist to also talk about how the imaginal exposure has changed for you over the course of therapy. Do you remember how you felt the first time you revisited and recounted this traumatic memory? How does it feel to do this today as compared to then? Has anything else changed about the memory or what the trauma means to your life now? Do you view the trauma experience differently than you did before?

Review of the Skills You Have Learned in This Program

Although we expect that you are feeling much better, we want to prepare you for "blips" in the future. There may be times in the future when it feels as though your PTSD symptoms are coming back or seem to be worsening. This might happen at times of stress, or maybe during times of change. Moving, getting a new job, getting married, having babies, children moving out, children getting married are all generally happy times, but they can be stressful. Your body has learned to react to extreme stress with PTSD symptoms, and you may notice some of these symptoms in the future. If you notice any of these symptoms, such as having an increase in intrusive thoughts or images of the trauma, withdrawing from others, avoiding trauma reminders, feeling very irritable, or having trouble sleeping, it will be important for you to pay attention to them. Pay attention to your habits and make sure you are doing what you have learned worked well to reduce your symptoms. Think about, and write down in this workbook, which skills worked best for you and what you need to remind yourself in the future.

After all the work you have done, it is important to review your progress in the program and take stock of the skills you have learned. You have spent a great deal of time and effort working with your therapist and doing hours of homework to help you process what happened to you during the trauma. In addition to repeatedly recounting the trauma memories in detail, you have spent a lot of time doing in vivo exposure exercises to help you approach people and situations that became frightening for you after the trauma or just felt unsafe somehow. This is a good time to think about how you are feeling now, what you found helpful or not helpful during treatment, what additional skills you need to learn, and your plans for the future.

Your therapist will use the in vivo hierarchy list you made together in session 2. When your therapist reads each item on the list, try to imagine yourself doing each of these things *right now* and what that would feel like. Your therapist will ask for your SUDS levels for each situation on the list if you did it now. You will then together go over the list and compare the ratings you made in session 2 to the ratings you made in the last session. We think you will be pleasantly surprised! For almost everyone going through this program, the SUDS levels go down a lot. Think about what that means for you. Think about how you did it, and what you learned about yourself and the world in the process of this program. Think about how hard it was, and how things have changed. Remember how hard you worked. You've earned those lower SUDS!

Look carefully at the list and the "before" and "after" ratings and see what you can learn. Which are the situations that went down the most? Talk about what you did to cause those changes. Is there anything that you rate near "0" now? We bet those are the situations you practiced a lot. Many people we work with wouldn't have thought when they started that it was possible to have some of these situations not bother them at all anymore. Which are some of the situations that didn't change as much? Why do you think these are still relatively anxiety provoking for you? What can you learn about those and what do you think you need to do? For many people, those will be the situations that they didn't practice as much. Just because you are finishing up with your therapist does not mean you will stop your exposure exercises. Just the opposite! You need to keep up your new good habits. If any of these situations are still bothering you, you need to work hard on them with in vivo exposure homework just like you did on the other situations during therapy. Your therapist can help you come up with a plan for tackling these situations. Also, you should be watchful for any increases in anxiety associated with the activities or situations you confronted during the therapy. If you see such an increase, what should you do? (Hint: what did you do that got you better?)

Please remember that what you have learned in this program is an approach, and it involves just that—*approaching*. Don't avoid something because it is upsetting. To get over it, there is no way to the other side except through it. You need to keep practicing this approach, keep facing your fears, and keep doing the work, even when it gets hard or scary—especially when it gets hard. You have worked so hard and been through so much to get to this place, but these are new habits that need continued practice. Some people at the end of therapy feel as though they are on a fence and could go either way at this point. We encourage you not to fall back into old habits of avoidance. It's like an exercise program to get into shape. If you work hard and achieve your goals but then stop exercising and eating well, you will slide back into old habits and may lose the gains you've made. One of our PTSD clients who was also recovering from her alcohol dependence said in the final session of her therapy, "I feel like I've been retrained and been given new skills and a new way to deal with things. It's just like my alcohol program—these two things go together—every day I need to just keep working this program the way I work my alcohol program." She was exactly right! And you, too, need to keep practicing exposure, staying with the upsetting memories, feelings, and situations that are realistically safe until you feel better about them.

We really want you to take stock of all that you've learned over this therapy and think about what helped you to feel better. Here are several questions to think about and discuss with your therapist:

- How did you accomplish these changes? What did you do in this therapy that brought about this difference?

- What have you noticed about your level of anxiety or discomfort in certain situations?

- What have you learned?

- What have you found most helpful to manage that anxiety and discomfort?

- Are there any problems that you are still concerned about? What do you think you need to do about these?

You should keep practicing the skills that you learned in therapy over the next several months very deliberately. If you run into problems, we encourage you to call your therapist for a booster session.

Graduation

We know that this type of work can be emotionally intense for both you and your therapist, so, not surprisingly, ending therapy can be difficult for people. Hopefully, you have come to trust your therapist and you have gotten through some intense work together. Take the time you need to say goodbye and think about what you have learned from this relationship. For many trauma survivors for whom trust was a huge issue, it can be very surprising that they have come to share such intimate details of a traumatic experience and have learned to trust their therapist so much. If this was true for you, this is a wonderful lesson for you. Isn't it good to know that you *can* trust someone again, that they can be there for you, and that you can let them be there for you? We hope you can apply this lesson to your other relationships or future relationships.

Again, take stock of what you have accomplished and what still needs some work. How helpful was the breathing relaxation for you? How often did you practice the imaginal exposure (listening to the tape) and how did it go for you? Did your feelings change? What made it easier? Did your thoughts change? How often were you able to practice the in vivo exposures? What more should you still work on? Importantly, what advice would you give someone you cared about who was thinking of going through this program?

In addition to being surprised that they could trust someone else, many people we have worked with are surprised that they could trust themselves, maybe again, maybe for the first time. We think in some ways, this is what this program is all about: gaining confidence in yourself and learning to trust that you can handle what life throws you. Congratulations! You should be very, very proud of yourself. We know what hard work this is, and you have made some great accomplishments. We are proud if this book, this program, and our experiences have helped you on this journey.

Good luck! Safe travels! Approach the rest of your life with confidence!

About the Authors

Barbara Olasov Rothbaum, PhD, is a professor in psychiatry at the Emory University School of Medicine in the Department of Psychiatry and Behavioral Sciences and director of the Trauma and Anxiety Recovery Program at Emory. Dr. Rothbaum specializes in research on the treatment of individuals with affective disorders, particularly focusing on anxiety and posttraumatic stress disorder (PTSD). She has won both state and national awards for her research, is an invited speaker internationally, authors scientific papers and chapters, has published and edited several books on the treatment of PTSD, and received the Diplomate in Behavioral Psychology from the American Board of Professional Psychology. She is the immediate past president of the International Society of Traumatic Stress Studies (ISTSS). Dr. Rothbaum is also a pioneer in the application of virtual reality to the treatment of psychological disorders.

Edna B. Foa, PhD, is a professor of clinical psychology in psychiatry at the University of Pennsylvania and director of the Center for the Treatment and Study of Anxiety. She received her PhD in clinical psychology and personality from the University of Missouri, Columbia, in 1970. Dr. Foa has devoted her academic career to studying the psychopathology and treatment of anxiety disorders, primarily PTSD, obsessive-compulsive disorder (OCD), and social phobia, and is currently one of the world's leading experts in these areas. Dr. Foa was the chair of the *DSM-IV* Subcommittee for OCD and cochaired the *DSM-IV* Subcommittee for PTSD. She has also been the chair for the Treatment Guidelines Task Force of the International Society for Traumatic Stress Studies.

Dr. Foa has published several books and over 250 articles and book chapters and has lectured extensively around the world. Her work has been recognized with numerous awards and honors. Among them are the Distinguished Professor Award under the Fulbright Program for International Exchange of Scholars; the Distinguished Scientist Award from the American Psychological Association, Society for a Science of Clinical Psychology; the First Annual Outstanding Research Contribution Award presented by the Association for the Advancement of Behavior Therapy; the

Distinguished Scientific Contributions to Clinical Psychology Award from the American Psychological Association; the Lifetime Achievement Award presented by the International Society for Traumatic Stress Studies; and the 2006 Senior Scholar Fulbright Award.

Elizabeth A. Hembree, PhD, is an assistant professor of psychology in psychiatry at the University of Pennsylvania School of Medicine. She is the director of training and the director of the Rape and Crime Victims Program in the Center for the Treatment and Study of Anxiety. Dr. Hembree received her PhD in clinical psychology from the University of Delaware in 1990. Her primary interest and research focus is the investigation and dissemination of cognitive behavioral treatment for PTSD. Dr. Hembree's scholarly publications include scientific articles and book chapters on the treatment of PTSD and OCD. She has been invited to speak internationally and has taught numerous workshops on the use of Prolonged Exposure Therapy (PE) for the treatment of PTSD.